*Revenge
of the Wolf*

Revenge of the Wolf

BRUCE GRAHAM

2025

All rights reserved. This book, or parts thereof,
may not be reproduced in any form without written
permissionfrom the publisher, except in the case of brief
quotations embodied in critical articles and reviews.

GPM Publishing
FreeRein Press

Copyright © 2025 by Bruce Graham

Illustrations by Kevin Ritchie with permission

First hardcover edition, 2025
ISBN: 979-8-9857865-6-9

First paperback edition, 2025
ISBN: 979-8-9857865-7-6

NO AI TRAINING: Without in any way
limiting the author's or publisher's exclusive rights
under copyright, any use of this publication to "train"
generative artificial intelligence (AI) technologies to generate
text is expressly prohibited. The author reserves all rights to
license uses of this work for generative AI training and
development of machine learning language modes.

1 3 5 7 9 10 8 6 4 2

First Printing

*"It is not the strength of the body
that counts, but the strength of the spirit."*

J.R.R. TOLKIEN

INTRODUCTION

In 1982 I took a fishing trip to northern Canada with several friends. The Canadian government had just opened this vast area to large-scale mining operations and to sportsmen seeking high adventure in an unspoiled wilderness. We were the first visitors to a new rustic fishing lodge in the Northwest Territories. It was a small no-frills operation, hundreds of miles from the nearest civilization. The only way to get to the lodge was by floatplane. After being there several days with excellent fishing success, I was awakened in the middle of the night by a commotion outside my cabin. As I peered out the window, I was shocked to see an enormous bear tearing up the camp. It had pushed over the outhouse and crushed open the plastic water pipes draining the outdoor shower area to lick out the soap coating the insides. It had torn off the screen door to the kitchen cabin and left deep claw marks on the main door trying to get to the food stored within. Fortunately, the cabin and its door were sturdily built. The other cabins where the guests resided, however, were made of flimsy plywood. I knew our cabin could easily be taken apart by this determined bear.

Bears have an extraordinary sense of smell. They can sense food from miles away. It was late April, and the ice had recently gone out. The bear had probably just come out of hibernation and was hungry. It likely had a bad disposition as well. We had been told by the camp manager not to keep any food in our cabins because of bears. I looked around and saw a large salami by the bed of one of my fellow fishermen. I saw the bear raise its nose in the air and sniff before turning toward our cabin. I screamed at the bear, but it kept coming. In fact, the bear and I made eye contact, and it was not deterred. My feelings turned to dread as the bear came relentlessly toward me. Why should the bear be satisfied with a salami when it could have a huge meal of me? When the bear was just a few yards away, Renny, our Cree fishing guide, jumped from out of nowhere onto the porch, raised a rifle, and sent three bullets into the bear's heart, killing it.

We were deeply indebted to our guide for his prompt, courageous action. Renny didn't think it was that big a deal. To him, it was simply another day on the job. However, he surprised us after shooting the bear by kneeling beside it and praying to its spirit in the Cree language. This reverent action was an ancient remnant of Cree hunter tradition. Renny said, "Just as in humans, there are good bears and bad ones. That bear knew to stay away from man, and he paid the price for his arrogance. It's unfortunate."

After Renny shot the bear, I gave him a Kansas City Royals baseball cap. He was overwhelmed and honored by the gift. To Renny, this was of greater significance than shooting the bear. What was a minor gift from me was a great symbol of friendship to him. He thought the KC logo on the hat, the place where I and my family lived, had profound meaning because I was sharing a part of my identity with him. It was like giving him a thousand dollars. He didn't know what baseball was, but he loved the "beautiful blue color."

Several days before the incident with the bear, Renny had come to me complaining of upper abdominal pain, which he had suffered with for years but was now getting worse. As a physician, I told him to stop chewing tobacco and gave him some medication that resolved his problem. The next day he was overjoyed and grateful to be cured of his pain. He told me he would take me to a lake no one knew about where I might be able to catch the biggest fish of the trip.

You get to know someone well when you spend ten hours a day in a boat together for fourteen days. Although Renny and I were from entirely different worlds, we formed an immediate lifelong friendship that went deeper than the superficialities of cultural difference. Renny was the most traditional Indigenous person I had ever dealt with. He had limited connections to the outside world. He had minimal education. English was not his primary language, and he spoke with a slow, deliberate Cree accent. He made his living as a fishing and hunting guide. In the winter he had a trapline that was over one hundred miles long from which he obtained furs to sell at a trading post in Churchill, Manitoba, a town on the shore of Hudson Bay. This small town on the tundra was the largest town he had ever been in.

We were discussing ancestry one day, and he discovered that I had Scottish heritage. He became excited and asked me if I knew Angus McDonald's family, since we were from the same "Scottish tribe." Evidently, Angus McDonald had many years before been a highly respected member of Renny's tribe, even though he was a white man married to a Cree woman. He had also been a close family friend to Renny's grandfather, whom Renny had idolized as a young boy. Renny had no concept of how big the world was or that Scottish ancestry was not that uncommon. He seemed to think there was more than a chance connection between us. He thought our connection must have been orchestrated by the Great Spirit for some purpose that we were not aware of yet. He told me that Angus McDonald, who had also been a "doctor," had given his grandfather a gift that had saved his life, and now I had given Renny a treasured gift. Renny's life in one of the most remote regions of North America had changed very little since his grandfather's day. Renny had more contact with white people, but otherwise his and his grandfather's lives were quite similar. Both earned a large portion of their livelihood by trapping furs in the winter.

When Renny, true to his word, later took me to his secret lake, I caught the largest northern pike of the trip. On our walk back to the boat, we came upon an enormous black rock that was conspicuously different from the surrounding gray granite of the region. It had a large flat surface the size of a small ice rink. The massive rock overlooked the expansive lake below and was situated next to a picturesque waterfall. Renny said the rock and this area were sacred ground. The black rock was, according to legend, a giant bear that the Great Spirit had turned into a rock. Renny was a member of the Bear Clan of the Cree tribe, who were responsible for the care of this sacred area. We climbed up on the rock, which to Renny was "a place of great power."

The rock became a stage for Renny to act out a true historical drama. He proceeded to tell me his grandfather Isha's harrowing story of being attacked by wolves; about Isha's deep friendship with his heroic lead sled dog, Atu; about Ishu's prophetic dreams; and about Angus McDonald, his friend and mentor. As he told me the story, he was dramatically animated, making quick movements and exaggerated facial expressions, jumping, and imitating the sounds of both animals and humans.

I could tell this was the way the Cree had passed down stories from one generation to the next through eons of time. I was honored that Renny had brought me to this sacred spot to tell me the story of his grandfather Isha and the revenge of a giant wolf. This book is based on Renny's story.

Bruce D. Graham

Revenge of the Wolf

The Omen

Isha talked with his wife, Cici, before going to bed about extending his current trapline. He had been thinking about it over the past year but had kept the idea to himself. "It sounds like a lot of work to me, and you'll be gone longer. I'm not sure I like the idea," Cici said. Isha was silent but couldn't get the thought out of his head. He'd been thinking about it too long to let it go that quickly. They both lay down in their bed and pulled the thick fur covers over them. Isha stared at the rafters of their cabin in deep thought for a while before drifting into sleep.

The man knelt in the snow, taking careful aim on a caribou with his Winchester lever-action rifle. He put his cheek against the wooden stock of the gun and tried to steady his grip. He was aiming for the heart. The animal had its side to the man, exposing the vulnerable part of the body. It was a long shot but one that the man had made many times before. This was the first time he had hunted in this region, and he didn't know the wildlife patterns in the area. He felt fortunate to have come across this caribou by chance. The man's sled-dog team was lying still, obediently following his command. He took a deep breath and let the air out slowly while steadying his rifle and slowly pulling the trigger. The gun fired with an uncomfortable kick to his shoulder. The caribou fell instantly. It was a perfect shot. The man felt a brief surge of elation while the dogs waited patiently for his next command. He and his dogs would eat well tonight. The man jogged over to inspect the fallen beast, a large bull with an impressive set of antlers.

As he was about to reach for his hunting knife to field dress the animal, he heard the long, distant howl of a wolf. He looked around but saw nothing. The only other sounds were those of his own rhythmic breathing and the wind softly whistling through the trees. He returned to the business at hand.

He heard another howl from the opposite direction but still saw nothing. He stood upright, motionless, listening intently. Soon there were howls all around him. Unsettled, he cocked his gun, putting another round in the chamber. He scanned the horizon and still saw nothing, although the howling continued unabated. He stood silently alert. After a few minutes, he spied several small figures on the horizon. They appeared as moving black objects against the snowy white background. He looked around and saw the same figures in the distance in all directions. He fixed his gaze upon these mysterious creatures for some time. He could tell the figures were running toward him. Slowly they came into focus. A large pack of wolves was approaching rapidly from all directions. He realized that being surrounded meant planning and not merely an inadvertent encounter. They seemed to have a singular purpose—to get the man. He was sure it wasn't the caribou carcass they wanted or they wouldn't be moving in so rapidly.

Unfortunately, he had left his dog team over a hundred yards away. He could tell from a distance that the dogs were fidgeting and obviously anxious in their harnesses. Wolves considered dogs a natural enemy to be killed on sight, and dogs instinctively understood this. Wolves usually avoid contact with humans. The man had never seen anything like this before, but he had to deal with blunt reality. He started running for his dog sled, but before he could reach it, the dogs suddenly bolted away at full speed despite his calls to them to return.

He was angered that the dogs he had put so much time and effort into training were now disobeying and leaving him when he needed them most. They knew they would be overtaken by the wolf pack within minutes unless they ran. They were no match for timber wolves, especially tied into their harnesses. The dogs quickly went out of sight. The man's heart sank, and his anger was replaced by fear. He knew that his chances of survival were slim without the dog team to make a fast getaway. He felt desperate and alone. He had no option but to turn in the opposite direction and run for the nearest cover, a steep embankment along the frozen lakeshore that harbored some trees. He hoped to make a stand there to fend off the rapidly closing wolf pack. His best chance was to get on top of the embankment and climb a tree, since wolves can't climb. After that, he would have to decide what to do next.

At the moment he was in the open in the middle of a large frozen lake. He began to run, but his pace was terribly slow since the snow was knee-deep. His snowshoes would have made his progress dramatically faster, but he had left them in the sled. His feet felt like lead blocks. Each step was like leaping over high hurdles to get his feet above the surface of the snow. No matter how hard he tried, he couldn't run faster. As he attempted to increase his speed, he tripped and fell headlong into the snow. The sudden slap in the face of the cold snow temporarily took his breath away. He quickly bounded to his feet, losing his hat in the process. He glanced back and saw the wolves closing rapidly.

As he ran, he came upon an unusual and strange sight. He saw a freshly killed wolf. It was a beautiful specimen, nearly totally white with a small amount of gray. He noticed a bloody bullet wound in the animal's chest. He thought, *Is another hunter close by?* He ran past the dead wolf, having no time to think about anything beyond his own survival. He yelled at the top of his voice, hoping that a hunter might hear him and come to his aid.

The wolves were gaining on the man. He kept running, but not fast enough. He looked back again and could now see their faces. Their malicious yellow eyes and their oversized white fangs were clearly visible. He could feel a flush of perspiration over his body as he tried to control his panic. He knew that death from a wolf attack would be an excruciating torture. He would be ripped apart, torn limb from limb, while still awake and aware.

The man reached the steep embankment on the lakeshore, slung his rifle strap over his shoulder, and frantically began to scramble up the side, where he thought he might be safe enough to make a stand with his trusty rifle and possibly climb a tree. He had only six shots left in the gun. There were far more than six wolves, but he hoped the loud noise of the rifle would scare away the remainder.

He finally felt that he was going to make it to safety away from the bloodthirsty pack that seemed determined to kill him. He pulled himself to the top of the bank, pushing his arms and head over the precipice and peering past the edge, ready to swing his legs up.

What he saw sent a shock wave through his body like an electric current. A mere ten yards away, more than twenty wolves waited for him, blocking his escape. His spirit felt bludgeoned as if by a sledgehammer to the chest. He let go of the snow-covered embankment and slid down.

Now he faced the main group of attackers head-on. They slowly closed in around him, baring their teeth and growling in low, guttural tones. He swung his rifle up and fired at the closest wolf. However, the shot didn't faze the wolf. It was still standing, growling and coming closer. He fired rapidly at several more wolves, again and again with no effect. Were his bullet shells blank? But he had just shot and killed a bull caribou. He fired again and found that he was out of shells. Still no effect on the wolves, nor did the near-deafening sound of the rifle cause fear. They continued to slowly close in on the man, ready to pounce. As the wolves approached, they bared their large fangs and the hair on their backs bristled. The man grabbed his rifle by the barrel and began to swing it as a club. He screamed as the pack jumped on him, not only from the front but also from the back, launching themselves as a group from the embankment above and knocking him to the ground. They began tearing and ripping his flesh to shreds. He tried defending himself with his arms and hands only to see them ripped away from his body in a bone-crushing dismemberment, covering the area with his blood. He screamed again, a visceral, blood-curdling sound of abject terror and pain that echoed for miles through the previously silent snow-covered land.

Isha sprang up from his bed, yelling. He was breathing rapidly as if he had just run a mile over rocky ground. He was exhausted from his terrible nightmare. His body was soaked with sweat. His hands were trembling uncontrollably.

"What's wrong, Isha?" said Cici.

"It was a horrible dream. I felt helpless. It was so real." Isha shook his head and ran his fingers through his tousled hair. He splashed some water on his face, slapping his cheeks several times to ensure his return to reality. He had never had a dream like this before and had never been prone to nightmares of any kind. He decided to take a walk outside his cabin to calm himself. He walked down to the lake, which was only a few yards away. It was still dark, but the moon was full, and its beautiful reflection gleamed on the surface of the lake. A gentle breeze whistled through the statuesque spruce and pine trees. He took a deep breath and absorbed the beautiful scene, which made him feel more relaxed. He loved the location of his cabin so close to the lake, which always gave him solace in trying times. Then he heard the long, haunting howl of a wolf far in the distance, which sent an alarming chill up his spine.

The Challenge and Preparation

Isha was a member of the Cree tribe of the Northwest Territories, Canada, living just a few miles south of the Arctic Circle. The date was 1913. He provided for his family by hunting, fishing, and trapping. Trapping furs was his main way of obtaining money to buy necessities at the local trading post, which was run by a white merchant. Since the location of this Cree village was so remote, contact with white society was limited. However, the turn of the twentieth century was beginning to make an impact on even the most remote regions of the Canadien far north. Manufactured goods from the outside world were beginning to make changes in Cree society. Modern tools, utensils, and other manufactured items made life easier. However, all the family's food was gleaned from the land. Their winter coats were made of fur that Isha obtained, since furs were more effective in combating the cold than any manufactured coats from the white world at the time. Most members of the tribe still wore buckskin clothing. Woolen and cotton apparel was just starting to be offered by the trading post. Isha's family was never hungry because he was a good provider, and he took great pride in this. Good providers had high prestige in the village, and Isha was considered one of the best.

Isha and Cici had a three-year-old child and were expecting a second within the year. His current trapline was productive and relatively close to the village, so he didn't have to travel far or be gone for long periods. With a new child on the way, extra money would be of great benefit to the family. Isha and Cici were practical people, so they were open to the use of new items that would improve the quality of their lives. Obtaining more money would require lengthening his trapline to cover more territory.

His present trapline was around twenty miles long, which was an average length for a Cree trapper. His plan was to extend it to a length of one hundred miles, which could potentially quadruple his income. He usually covered the trapline on foot on snowshoes since trapping was done in the winter, when an animal's fur is thickest and therefore most valuable. Isha was rarely gone more than three days when checking his traps. He had built a shelter at the end of the trapline trail, where he spent the night as needed or if there was a storm.

Beyond this shelter to the north lay an area he had never explored. This region, the Seal River country, had seemed strangely foreboding to Isha ever since he had been a young boy trapping with his father.

At the end of their twenty-mile trapline, he would invariably stare with curiosity at the vast area to the north. This place had a mysterious quality that was somehow intriguing. It looked much different from the area where he lived. Everything seemed larger. The lake appeared like an ocean with huge, jagged boulders and large trees surrounding it. It was so unlike Lake Kashapon, where he lived, which had shallow bays filled with lily pads, wild rice, and sandy beaches perfect for lounging and basking in the sun in the less than four weeks of summer during which it was occasionally warm. The entire region to the north, as well as the massive lake, seemed dangerous. Next to the shelter his father had built, a large boulder sat at the top of a small ravine that led down to the lakeshore. The boulder and the ravine seemed like a gateway to the region beyond.

In a strange way, this region now loomed as a challenge to Isha's courage and proficiency as a hunter and trapper. It beckoned him to face the fear of the unknown. It seemed that he had something to prove, maybe because his father had been killed in the region to the north or maybe because neither his father nor anyone else had trapped the area in the winter. His father had frequently talked about trapping this region someday but had never done so because of his premature death.

All Isha knew was that the region to the north was calling him. He didn't know if it was for good or evil, but he was determined to find out. More than just earning extra money for his family, he thought of this region where most villagers were afraid to go as an adversary to be conquered.

Strings of complicated interconnecting lakes and swamps intermingled with dense forests were the hallmarks of this vast area. There were no established trails, making access difficult for humans. For these reasons there was a high likelihood that large amounts of furs could be obtained if he could get to them. He had heard that this area was dangerous because "evil spirits" inhabited it. Some villagers thought a demon monster called the Wendigo, prominent in Cree legends, lived there. However, Isha thought the rumors had started because of the rough terrain creating difficulty of access and because people wanted to make excuses not to go farther away and work harder.

To extend Isha's trapline would mean investing in a sled and a dog team. Dogs were expensive and could be paid for with money or by trading goods and services. However, maintenance and training of the dogs were another matter. Feeding the dogs would require him to kill one or two extra caribou or moose and catch more fish every year. Isha felt confident that he could do these things without much difficulty. Properly training dogs to follow complex commands and work as a team took a great amount of time and effort. He'd had some experience with this as a younger man and had always enjoyed it. When he was a young boy, his father had made him a flat-based toboggan with an upturned front that was pulled by several eight- to twelve-month-old puppies. The young Isha thought this was great fun. He was able to follow his father's dog sled around the frozen lake and through trails in the bush for short distances.

At the end of winter, when the trapping season was done, Isha obtained six dogs and a seventh dog named Atu who had more experience pulling a sled. Although some teams had more dogs and others less, he thought seven would be the perfect number. If he had more dogs, he would have to carry more food for them, making the sled too heavy and not leaving enough room for pelts over a long trek. It would also take more time and effort to properly train more dogs. Fewer than seven dogs would not generate enough power and endurance to pull the sled long distances. Isha had a plan to train the seven dogs to a degree that would make them as strong as a larger team. The team required a capable lead dog since that dog would be in front of the others alone. The dogs he'd bought were already healthy, but he thought he could get them in even better physical condition with a little work and improved nutrition.

The previous owner of the dogs, a man named Soskin, was a well-respected trapper and hunter who was known to be a no-nonsense rough taskmaster. He knew how to properly train sled dogs and prepare them for the rigors of a subarctic winter. While showing the dogs to Isha in the crowded, undersized fenced enclosure, Soskin kicked them and struck them with a large stick to get them out of the way so he could show Isha the entire pack. One dog jumped on Soskin, thinking he was going to feed them. Soskin kicked the dog in the chest, catapulting it into the air like a football. It landed several yards away, yelping and running toward the back of the enclosure.

Soskin said, "That dog is the stupidest of the bunch, but he's a fast runner."

The dogs in the enclosure recognized Soskin as their source of food, but they were wary of him as a potential source of pain. However, their hunger overcame their fear, so most of the dogs surrounded him, begging for food. He tried to convince Isha to buy a trained lead dog that was dramatically more expensive than a standard sled dog.

Isha declined as he carefully looked around at the pack. He noticed a large dog on the other side of the pen cowering at the sight of the big stick, as if the dog had firsthand experience with it.

Isha pointed and asked, "What's the name of the big dog on the other side?"

"Oh, that's Atu. He's strong enough, but he hasn't panned out as well as I expected him to. He's hesitant to follow commands, even when kicked or given the whip. The other dogs fall into line quickly after a few knocks, but not Atu. It's not that he's dumb like some dogs. I think he's just stubborn. I'll give you a discount on him."

Isha was impressed not only with the dog's size but with the way Atu carried himself around the other dogs. They gave Atu a wide berth. Isha had noticed the big dog gazing at him from the edge of the compound as soon as he entered the enclosure, which he thought unusual for a dog. Isha and Soskin walked over to the big dog. Atu lowered his head to Isha's feet, as if he were a sensitive dog who had been mistreated in the past. While he had his head bent, he gazed up at Isha with a depth that Isha had never seen in a dog before. The look was almost human and seemed to be trying to communicate, as if saying, *Please take me and you won't be disappointed.* Isha knelt and extended his hand to the big dog. Atu initially recoiled from Isha's advance but quickly became more relaxed as Isha rubbed his head.

Soskin said, "You'd better be careful; you might get bit." But Isha had a good feeling about this big dog. He could detect deep personality and character, implying that Atu was more intelligent than the average dog. He also thought this dog was highly sensitive. Harsh punishment would not be the best way to get the most out of a dog like this. Yet Atu seemed to be respected by other dogs, which was uncommon for a sensitive dog. Respect was not easy to obtain in this half-wild group of sled dogs of the far north, who tend to respect only raw and savage power. Isha suspected that there was an underlying dynamic around the big dog that was not obvious.

"Oh, I don't think he'll bite me." Isha could tell Soskin was not in the habit of petting his dogs and kept his relations with them strictly business. Isha thought that if given a chance, the big dog would make the perfect lead. He moved his hand to Atu's body and slowly rubbed the dog's back. Atu now seemed to enjoy being caressed by this new man as he brushed up against Isha, asking for more attention. Atu had never felt such a pleasant sensation from a human. He had never experienced kindness or love before. This was a new sensation, and his deep need for it had never been fulfilled before.

Atu

Atu had been weaned from his mother much earlier than most puppies because of his large size, but he was still quite vulnerable because of his lack of maturity. He was placed in the pen with the adult dogs despite his youth. He missed his mother and littermates greatly but didn't dare cry for fear of showing weakness that the adult dogs would take advantage of.

Even at such a young age, Atu showed that he was clever and adaptable. To ensure his safety while still young, he would give small pieces of his meager food ration to the two largest dogs in the pen, Ashiny and Sohkekan. They weren't the smartest dogs around, but their size served as good protection while Atu was growing up. The two big dogs didn't do much but simply hang around Atu. However, their mere presence associated them with the puppy, who was therefore protected even though the two big dogs didn't know what they were doing except waiting to be fed. Ashiny and Sohkekan seemed to know that Atu had something they lacked: intelligence. For the most part Atu got along well with the other dogs and was treated like a younger sibling while growing up, thanks in part to his two big friends. Eventually Atu grew larger and stronger than his two older protectors as well as the others.

Despite Atu's large size, Soskin's dog pen was a dangerous place to be, with continuous fights and squabbles over food and dominance. Soskin usually did nothing to stop the commotion among his dogs and let nature take its brutal course. However, he intervened if a fight involved his valuable and expensive lead dog, Lolo, and would beat any dog that attacked Lolo with a large stick or his long caribou-leather whip. For several years, Lolo was looked upon as the dominant dog in the pen, not only because of his viciousness and large size but also because of Soskin's protection. Lolo frequently bullied and harassed other dogs that were smaller and weaker for no reason except to show his power and to steal food. A gang of others followed his lead in harassing the more timid dogs, nipping at them, stealing their food, and making their lives miserable. This frequently led to weakness and malnutrition in the oppressed dogs. A weakened dog was often set upon by Lolo's gang and killed. Occasionally Soskin had to kill a severely injured dog to "put it out of its misery." The rule in the pack was to obey the strong and take advantage of the weak.

When Atu matured, Lolo and his gang looked upon him with suspicion as a potential rival for dominance within the pen. The most threatening aspect of Atu was not his size or fighting ability but his intelligence and inherent confidence, which gave him leadership capability. The gang sensed Lolo's growing animosity toward Atu and began to nip and harass Atu, demanding immediate subservience. Atu bared his teeth and snarled at Lolo's minions but never retaliated. He knew Lolo was the source of his harassment, and he realized that fighting multiple battles with lesser dogs would be unproductive and possibly dangerous if he had to fight the whole gang at once. The harassment grew in frequency and intensity until it became a near-hourly occurrence. Ashiny and Sohkekan were of no help because they were oblivious to the situation. Although they were big dogs, they weren't particularly bright and thus presented no threat to Lolo and his gang. Atu couldn't go anywhere within the enclosure without a growl, a nip, or an attempt to steal his food. The tension within the enclosure was palpable. Atu knew the present situation was not sustainable and would only become worse. What he didn't want was to be set upon by Lolo and his gang of many dogs all at once. This would present a high risk of injury as well as a possible beating by Soskin.

Eventually Atu had enough. In the middle of the night, while Soskin and most of the dogs were sleeping, Atu strolled over to Lolo. He chose this time to avoid detection and potential punishment by the master. Lolo slowly opened his eyes to see Atu close to his face, snarling and showing his fangs. Unexpectedly awakening to an extreme threat caused him to panic. Before he knew how to respond, Atu struck with lightning-like speed and precision, crushing and ripping one of Lolo's ears in two. Lolo screeched and ran to the fence. Atu raced after him, slashing a deep, bloody gash in Lolo's thigh and then knocking him down with a heavy blow to the body. Atu loomed over

Lolo as the injured dog cowered below his feet. The other dogs were astounded by the ferocity and suddenness of the attack. The darkness somehow created a multiplying effect of greater shock and fear. The entire pack gathered around Lolo and Atu. When Lolo attempted to move, Atu opened his jaws, pressing his large canine fangs next to Lolo's face. Lolo got the message that any movement to escape would lead to severe, irreparable damage. He gave a slight whine and tucked his tail between his legs to indicate submission. Atu did not attempt to kill or permanently injure the other dog, even though he had the capability to do so, and Lolo knew it. Atu simply walked away.

The next day Soskin noticed blood in the enclosure. His valuable lead dog was limping, with obvious injuries. Soskin became enraged and began yelling at the dogs as if they could understand or speak to him. He grabbed his large stick and started hitting the ground in anger. He took Lolo out of the compound and tied him to a tree on a long leash to prevent any further injury. To Lolo and the rest of the pack, it seemed that Lolo was being imprisoned as punishment rather than for his own protection.

Lolo's ear was never the same. It flopped down to the side while the other, normal ear stayed erect. This was a permanent reminder to the pack of who was truly in charge, and they left Atu alone. From then on Soskin's dog enclosure was less chaotic. Harassment of smaller and weaker dogs stopped. Lolo's gang looked to Atu for leadership and direction, but Atu ignored them. If they came too close, he gave a low growl until they went away.

Soskin's dogs had to live under the strict tyranny of a master who meted out punishment for the slightest infractions. It wasn't uncommon for Atu to unexpectedly feel the sharp sting of the whip as a message to increase speed while pulling the sled with the other dogs. Atu and the other dogs didn't understand the purpose of the whip. They increased their speed to get away from the pain caused by the master behind them. Most of the dogs gave immediate subservience, but Atu resented the severe treatment and occasional punishment inflicted on him and the others. He refused to work hard in the face of cruelty. He did the bare minimum with reluctance and no extra effort. Atu felt that Soskin did not deserve his respect and total obedience. There was no such thing as a kind word or a pat on the head for a job well done, only retribution for error or not reacting quickly enough to commands. However, he was happy to be a member of the dog team since he was driven by instinct to run with the pack, despite Lolo being the lead dog.

Atu dreamed of something better, a life he didn't think existed. He thought life outside the human world was even more threatening and dangerous. He had seen the slaughtered carcasses of various animals placed in the dog sled by the ultimate predator—man. He occasionally heard the howling of wolves in the distance. He recognized the similarity of their calls to those of dogs but also realized that they were different. He had never seen a wolf and was curious about what they looked like. When hearing the howls of the wolves, fear ran through the dog pack. They instinctively knew that wolves were dangerous and mortal enemies.

"I think I'll take this big one here, Atu," said Isha.

Atu was part Alaskan malamute and part Siberian husky. He had the positive assets of both breeds and none of the negatives. He had the size and strength of a large malamute and the speed, agility, and endurance of a husky. He was big and strong but relatively inexperienced at four years old. He had been trained to follow commands and to pull the sled but had never run in the all-important lead position. A good lead dog was essential to the success of the dog team. Some dogs didn't have the intelligence or confidence to ever be a lead dog. Others didn't have the strength and endurance. It took a combination of all these attributes to be a good lead dog. In addition, the lead needed to be respected as a head of the pack, which was an intangible quality that could often be difficult to assess. It took a discerning eye to pick a good lead dog for a sled team.

After purchasing the seven dogs, Isha placed them in his enclosed dog compound, where he made an individual small house for each dog. He filled these kennels with grass and hay for insulation. The shelters were a departure from the standard care of dogs in the village. The enclosure itself was much less crowded and larger than Soskin's, giving each dog more individual space and less chance for tension to build. Dogs were usually kept outside no matter what the conditions; thus, the shelters gave them an added sense of comfort and security. Isha fed them far better than their previous owner. They immediately knew that he was a dramatically different type of master. For once they weren't hungry after a meal and didn't have to fight over leftover scraps.

Atu was excited about his new environment. He was away from the continuous fighting and squabbling that had been part of his previous life. He was also happy that the new master had bought Ashiny and Sohkekan. The other dogs were all agreeable animals that he liked, and none had been in Lolo's gang. His new master was a dramatic change for the better. Sled dogs of the north were bred to work. A job and a duty made them feel worthwhile and happy. He couldn't wait to get to work for his new master. He could feel that a new bright day had begun.

Isha quickly developed a bond with all the dogs, but especially with Atu. He felt that there was something about Atu that Soskin hadn't noticed. Atu responded enthusiastically to any special attention from Isha. He became a completely different dog, thriving on the loving attention and seeming more playful and happier. Isha took time to observe Atu's behavior around the other dogs. He noticed that Atu commanded respect even from the more mature ones. Atu was not prone to biting or fighting to obtain the deference given him. He was larger than the other dogs, which may have been one of the reasons. However, he had a calm, confident disposition that made him a perfect choice for a leader of the dog team.

Atu showed a high degree of athleticism not commonly seen in dogs. Isha noted that when he threw a bone into the pen, Atu was able to leap into the air to get the bone before the other dogs. The bone would then be left uncontested with Atu. Because of his commanding presence, the others dared not challenge the big dog. Isha noted that there was much less fighting and squabbling among this group of dogs than among most others. In large part, this was due to Atu's stabilizing influence along with Isha's care and adequate feeding.

It became apparent that Atu understood commands much more quickly than most dogs. In short, he was faster, stronger, and smarter than the other dogs. Isha realized he had found a valuable gemstone on a gravel beach, a truly rare find that had gone unnoticed.

Isha played with the dogs in his spare time. He would go into the pen with the dogs, give them treats, and roll around on the ground with them like a child playing with friends. It was rare for dogs to be treated so well in the village, where they were considered strictly work animals. The concept of keeping a dog as a pet was uncommon and was felt to be childish, something that men grew out of as they matured. However, Isha was an independent spirit and didn't mind what other people thought of him.

All seven dogs, but especially Atu, began to blossom. One could almost detect a smile on Atu's face when he was being given attention. Isha would bring Atu with him on minor outings and errands in the village. The other dogs saw this special relationship between Atu and their master and more readily accepted Atu's leadership. Atu was tentatively tolerated throughout the community because he was with Isha. However, the villagers thought it a little odd for a man to walk around the village with a dog. Most people thought Isha had a kind heart, a quality from his childhood that had never gone away, similar to a chronic disability or disease he was afflicted with and could not control. Many people thought it had to do with his father's untimely death.

It was unusual for sled dogs to be friendly because they usually had to fight for food and dominance. As a rule, they were not treated particularly well by their masters, who considered them half wild and potentially dangerous, akin to wolves. Most men with sled dogs carried whips or clubs to enforce their commands. The dogs were always hungry, not starved but fed just enough to do their work. Isha's dogs were different. He believed that inadequate feeding of dogs led to less unity of the pack as well as less strength and endurance. Unity of purpose would be needed to pull his sled over long distances. He also felt that the dogs would work harder and learn more quickly if they were treated better.

Isha made a sled frame out of willows and pine saplings. The body of the sled and the handlebar were lashed together with caribou tendons boiled in water so they would shrink and tighten when they dried. Heated pine resin was placed over the dried tendons for further strength. The sides and base of the sled were made of moose hide, softened by rubbing with animal fat and brain tissue so that it wouldn't crack in the cold temperatures. The stretched hides were lashed to the wooden frame. The sled runners were made of cut willows soaked with boiling water and bent at the front end into a slight curl. Isha coated the runners with moose fat to make them run smoothly through the snow and avoid ice buildup, which would cause more drag.

Sled-Dog Training

Atu could hardly believe his good fortune when Isha hooked him into the leather lead-dog harness. He had finally been placed in the position he'd been longing for, and he was determined not to disappoint his kind new friend and master. The other dogs instinctively followed Atu's lead without question. They loved running together while pulling the sled. It was their version of running with a hunting pack, something they were genetically programmed to do as predator pack animals like wolves, their distant wild cousins.

Isha began the tedious and time-consuming process of training the dogs with his new sled. The dogs were strong and willing to please but still inexperienced. They were easily distracted. When they saw a rabbit or some other animal, they tended to lose concentration and

chase it. Isha taught them to stay focused on the task of pulling the sled and following Atu's lead. Overall, they were doing better than he had expected. Atu needed training as well since this was his first time as lead dog, but he learned quickly.

Isha yelled commands for the team to go right (HHAA), left (GGEE), go (MUSH), and stop (HO). There were also many more complicated commands such as stay, lie down, circle, and run faster or slower. Isha would jump off the sled, grab Atu, and pull him to the left or right while giving the command. He did this repeatedly with the other dogs as well, but they weren't as quick to learn. Isha reinforced their good behavior with treats of dried fish and a pat on the head. This was approach to training was the opposite of that used by Soskin and most other Cree sled-dog masters.

Once or twice per week Isha would take the dogs to an open field close to the village and give them "play time" without the sled. It was a time of loose fun while learning for Isha and the dogs. Isha would run at the head of the pack and then bark out a command. He would immediately stop and turn to see the dogs' response. He would then progress to numerous more complex commands. This was fun for the dogs as well as for Isha and reinforced training in a different, fun way while creating a bonding experience. Some of the villagers thought this was a little crazy. However, none could deny Isha's status as the best provider of the tribe as well as a good husband and father.

During the summer months Isha ran the dogs with the sled daily over a field of grass, which was far more difficult for the dogs than pulling over snow. This strengthened the dogs and increased their endurance. No one had ever heard of training dogs in the summer months before. The villagers watched Isha training the dogs on grass in disbelief. But Isha knew that strength needed to be built slowly over time to achieve its maximum benefit. He tested each individual dog, having it pull the sled solo for short sprints to build speed. This also gave each dog individual training in following Isha's commands. He realized that some dogs learned better with individual attention than with the pack. This also built a relationship between him and each dog. By doing solo training, Isha was able to identify each dog's strengths and weaknesses. He knew that one day the rigorous training would pay off and indeed might save his life. After a good run pulling the sled, Isha routinely rewarded the dogs with a treat of dried fish.

Isha placed large stones in the sled to slowly increase its weight daily. He eventually placed more weight in the sled than he expected to ever carry. Eventually the dogs were pulling a sled filled to the top with large boulders across grass with relative ease. Isha then had the dogs pull the boulder-laden sled farther and farther. This was even more difficult since it was done in the summer heat, which most sled dogs were not used to. This improved their stamina and endurance even more. After a rigorous training session Isha often took the dogs to the nearby lake to cool off and play in the water.

Over time Isha was able to distinguish the physical and emotional characteristics of each dog. The dogs were placed in pairs, with Atu alone in front because he was by far the strongest and smartest of the dogs. The two next-strongest dogs, Ashiny and Sohkekan, meaning "rock" and "strong," respectively, were placed closest to the sled. They weren't the brightest of the group, but they were strong and hardworking. They were next to Isha so he could easily correct them. In the position next to the sled, strength is more important than intelligence. They could easily follow the dogs in front while pulling the heaviest load. They weren't responsible for initiating quick turns or following complex commands.

The two youngest dogs were the fastest and were placed behind Atu so that they could follow his lead. Nicimos, meaning "sweetheart," and Jabweh, meaning "cutie," were exuberant, happy dogs, always wanting to play but tending to be distracted more often than the others. The two behind them were steady and reliable, not as fast or strong as the others but with excellent endurance. Tipiskaw, meaning "moon," and Poslite, meaning "sun," could always be relied upon, like the celestial bodies they were named for. The dogs who were paired as running mates on the team seemed to bond with each other, but they all got along well within their enclosure. Atu was friendly but remained somewhat aloof from the other dogs. He knew what it took to be respected as a leader. His primary allegiance was to Isha.

After a little less than a year had passed, Isha was optimistic about his new dog team. He thought the training of the dogs had been great fun rather than a hard and tedious chore, as most village dog masters thought. He relished working with his new "little brothers," as he called them. Isha couldn't wait for the snow to come so he could really tell how much the dogs had progressed.

After the first snowfall Isha took the team on a run close to the village. He and the dogs slowly traveled over the open snow-covered field where they had practiced so many times in the past. Then they came to the entrance of a trail that led into the bush. "MUSH MUSH MUSH YA!" Isha yelled, giving the command for maximum speed. The sled exploded through the trail entrance. Isha felt that he was flying. This was the fastest and strongest dog team he had ever encountered. He felt exhilarated as the speed made the wind rush against his face. The sled was going so fast that he was afraid to jump off for fear of losing his footing and being dragged. The dogs felt that they were hardly pulling anything since they were used to pulling the heavily laden sled on grass. Isha was now confident that this team would be ready for anything once the lakes froze and the river systems became his highways. Little did he know that all the training and preparation of the dogs would become invaluable to him in the future.

With the change to colder weather and snow, Isha could see a change in the dogs' behavior. They were more energetic and happier, almost giddy. When unleashed from the sled harness, they would jump into snowbanks and roll around like playing children. These dogs were bred for the cold. Alaskan malamutes and Siberian huskies have two different and separate layers of thick fur specifically adapted for frigid weather, like timber wolves. They relished the cold as much as they detested the heat.

Cici

Isha's wife, Cici, was a pretty woman with fine, delicate features. She wore her long black hair in two braids. Brightly colored strips of ribbon were sewn onto her cotton calico blouse newly acquired from Angus McDonald's trading post. Cotton and wool clothing from the white world were recent additions to the apparel of the tribe. These were highly favored and fashionable garments, especially among the young women. The new apparel was more comfortable, especially during the summer months, than the traditional heavier and warmer buckskin clothing.

Cici was short but athletic and noticeably strong for such a small-framed woman. Reserved but confident, she managed her household well for long periods while Isha went hunting, exhibiting a strong independent and practical nature. She was kind and doting to their three-year-old son. Isha considered her a wonderful wife and mother and felt fortunate to have her. Their personalities seemed to fit perfectly. Both were easygoing people who got along with everyone in the village. Cici frequently thought about the exciting times when Isha had been courting her with the approval of her father. She recalled him being reserved but confident, like her. She remembered swimming alone with Isha in the lake far from the village, taking short canoe trips, and fishing. They'd had on-shore lunches of delicious fish and berries. However, her life had now changed dramatically. As the wife of a good man and a mother, she was happier than she had ever been. She felt that she was in the natural cycle of life where she was meant to be. She was grateful to the Great Spirit for having blessed her in such a way. She was not enthusiastic about Isha taking on a new trapline in unknown territory that would take him away for longer periods. She understood that Isha's energetic and ambitious spirit drove him to make more money for the family; however, she was content with the way things were rather than adding more work and effort to their lives. She was willing to support him in whatever he wished to do but still opposed the new adventure, especially in view of his strange dream.

Cici had been working on new winter gear for Isha for nearly a year to prepare him for long periods in the bush in extremely cold temperatures. With the help of her mother, who lived in a cabin fifty yards from her, Cici made a coat of moose hide with an interior lining of caribou fur. A shawl and hood of wolverine fur were draped over the shoulders, back, and neck of the coat. She made a hat with earflaps and mittens, each from two layers of beaver fur, as the fur is waterproof. She used a double layer of otter skin with fur on the inside to make mukluks that extended up to the knees. As a semiaquatic mammal, the otter also has waterproof fur. She placed thick caribou moss inside the mukluks for insulation and to absorb moisture. She made Isha's trousers from a double layer of caribou hide.

The hat, mittens, and mukluks were embroidered with beautiful colorful beadwork designs considered to bring power and good luck. The designs of the beadwork were insignias of their tribe and specific clan within the tribe. There was also a design of yellow and red lightning bolts that was specific to Isha. The three pieces of apparel, embroidered with beadwork, were made to bring the most power to the areas of his body where he would need it the most: his head, hands, and feet. The fine thread and the metal needles used for the embroidery were obtained from the trading post.

Making such clothing took a considerable amount of time. The hides were stitched together with the tendons of caribou, boiled in water to make them more pliable. When they dried, they shrank, drawing the pieces of the coat closer and making it stronger. This was far more durable than the thread that white people used for their coats. The needle holes where the soft tendon was passed through the thick animal hide were made with hand awls of bone and antler, as were the large needles used to sew the hide. The village women frequently gathered to work together, making their jobs less tedious. Cici liked working with her friends. They would sing, laugh, and talk about their families, children, and the village. This made the job of making clothing an event that the women looked forward to and enjoyed.

Angus and Aingan

Some pieces of apparel made by white people were superior to traditional Native clothes. To complete the preparation for the long trek into the bush, Isha walked through the village with Atu to Angus McDonald's trading post, which was located two miles away on a small river.

Angus had set up his trading post just outside the village many years ago. He had married a Cree woman and settled in the village when Isha was a small boy. Angus's trading post was the nearest outpost of civilization for hundreds of miles. Cree people from all over the vast Canadian bush came there to buy modern goods and tools. The river where the trading post was located gave access to other river systems, eventually connecting to the outside world, though reaching any kind of white civilization took weeks or even months by canoe or dog sled. The rivers eventually connected to the huge Lake Winnipeg to the south and the city of Winnipeg on the lake's southern end. The river systems also connected to the small trading town of Churchill, Manitoba, located to the east on Hudson Bay much closer than the city of Winnipeg. Churchill was where Angus received most of the goods for his trading post and where he sold his furs.

After Angus set up his trading post, life in the village vastly improved. Before then, half the hunters had used single-shot smoothbore muskets or bows and arrows to bring down game. Metal pots and pans for cooking made home life much easier. The use of canvas tarps for shelter helped hunters and trappers greatly because canvas was much lighter and easier to work with than heavy animal hides stitched together. Metal fishing hooks and thin braided fishing line made harvesting fish more reliable.

The entire economy of the village revolved around the fur trade, of which Angus was the hub. In Isha's grandfather's day, the tribe had occasionally experienced times of great famine when the hunting was not good. During these hard times the very young and the elderly were at higher risk of dying. Within one generation, the way of life in the village had dramatically changed for the better because of these new connections to the faraway outside world.

Angus knew Isha well and had seen him grow up. He recognized that Isha had a kind heart and an easygoing personality. Isha was naturally drawn to Angus because of his good nature as well as his wealth of experience. Angus had been a close friend and partner in the fur business with his late father.

Isha's father had died when Isha was eleven years old, which had affected him greatly. He had been close to his father, who had taught him to hunt and trap. Although he had a loving and supportive mother, Isha became somewhat of a loner after his father's death. By age sixteen he had already become an accomplished hunter and had his own trapline that he had inherited from his father. Since he was single with no family to support, he gave a large portion of the meat he hunted to villagers who had difficulty supporting themselves. When he was twenty-two he built his own cabin by the lake and began courting Cici.

After his father's death and prior to going out on his own, Isha helped his uncle Aingan with hunting and trapping. Isha looked up to his father's friend Angus and his father's brother Aingan as life mentors but mainly kept his own counsel.

Aingan was very different from Isha's father or Angus, who were both happy and good-natured. Aingan had a stern and taciturn personality. He was all business and rarely smiled; however, he was loyal and could always be trusted. Nearly six feet eight inches tall, Aingan was much larger than any other man in the village. He had huge, muscular shoulders and arms. His gorilla-like hands dwarfed those of most normal-sized men. One finger of Aingan's was the size of two of Isha's. He had a deep and noticeable scar on his face that he had received from a wounded moose while hunting with Isha, who was then eleven years old. Aingan shot the large bull and was initially surprised when the moose went down because he didn't believe he'd shot accurately. He thought, *Sometimes you just get lucky.* When he straddled the moose to field dress the fallen beast, the moose suddenly stood up, having been only wounded and stunned. The moose violently shook his head, and one of its antlers gashed Aingan's face to the bone. Aingan dropped his knife as the moose rose to its feet, and the moose charged into the forest with Aingan holding on to its neck. Most men would have let go and fallen to the ground to avoid further injury, but Aingan was now enraged and wanted deadly vengeance. He gave a bloodcurdling yell as the moose hurtled through the tangled brush. Aingan, with his thick arms and legs wrapped around the moose's neck, strangled the animal, constricting its airway until it fell to the ground several hundred yards from where it had originally been shot.

Isha witnessed the entire event. He ran through the thick underbrush after his uncle and the moose, yelling for his uncle, who he thought might be in mortal danger. He finally caught up with Aingan, still strangling the now downed and dead moose. Aingan eventually stood up, blood pouring from the gash on his face, and began laughing while looking at his terrified nephew. The wound on his face extended from his forehead to his chin. The deep portion of the wound was white, exposing the facial bone. His eyebrow and portions of his scalp, nose, and lip were cut nearly in half. Aingan walked to the front of the dead moose and kicked it violently in the nose as he spit blood out of his mouth. He then told his young nephew to fetch the butcher knife so they could finish what they had started. Aingan field dressed the moose, not bothering to care for his deep facial wound, oblivious to the blood actively dripping on the ground and his clothes as he skinned and quartered the giant beast. After several hours, when the job was completed, Aingan's face and shirt were red with blood. His shirt was torn to shreds, and he had multiple smaller bleeding lacerations on his arms and scalp from the branches tearing at him as the moose ran through the brush. Isha was appalled at the sight of Aingan, still slowly dripping blood, standing over the skinned carcass of the huge moose with its internal organs and entrails spilling onto the bloody ground. Aingan could tell that his young nephew was shocked by the gory scene.

Aingan said, "Are you afraid of the sight of a little blood, nephew?" Isha stared at him in silence. Aingan then broke out in laughter, showing a large, lacerated smile with several absent teeth.

Isha had recently started working with his uncle after his father's death. Isha thought, *What kind of man is this? He's half animal. He has not even the slightest resemblance to my father.* However, he knew Aingan was an excellent woodsman whom he could learn a lot from. He also knew Aingan was dedicated to his care and welfare in the absence of his father. Isha thought, *I pity the man who gets on the wrong side of Uncle Aingan. He might forget he's part human.* There were rumors in the village that Aingan had received the scar from a bear that he had strangled to death with his bare hands. Aingan did nothing to dispel this rumor.

Aingan was married to Angus's wife's sister, a short, plump woman with a sweet, outgoing, and happy disposition. She had a continuous smile on her face. She frequently sang to herself while working at home and was the opposite of Aingan in all respects. When standing beside her husband, she came to just above his waist. Aingan had married late in life, and it was thought that he had just become tired of cooking for himself and decided to find a wife. Aingan at one time had had a dog sled team, but it hadn't worked out well because of his size and weight. The dogs always had difficulty pulling him, and he would have needed an army of dogs to effectively pull him and an extra load. Most people thought him a bit scary because of his appearance and personality, but he was respected because of his hunting and trapping skills. Aingan had few close friends besides Isha and Angus. He generally kept to himself.

Angus was older and had retired from strenuous activity in the wilderness. The old Scotsman had a lucrative business running the trading post, especially since it was the only one for hundreds of miles. He was a short, stocky man with a gray beard and a round, happy, ruddy face. He wore a tam-o'-shanter plaid wool hat, the classic head covering from his country of birth. The unique, vibrant red-and-yellow plaid was the insignia of the McDonald clan, which Angus was a member of.

Angus had grown up herding sheep in northwest Scotland close to the Irish Sea. He'd become an expert at an early age in raising and training the sheep dogs that aided him in his work as a young shepherd. The care of the large flock was his primary youthful responsibility. It was a solitary, lonely job, so he grew quite close to his dogs. At the time he identified with young King David in the Bible since he too had been a shepherd in his youth and spent long hours tending the sheep alone except for his dogs and the almighty. Instead of disliking his life, Angus loved the solitude and natural beauty of the Scottish Highlands. His parents gave him an education and made sure he was familiar with the teachings of Christianity. Since he was given significant responsibility as a boy, he grew into a confident and resourceful man.

He was orphaned at the age of fourteen when both parents died of a sudden and unexpected illness less than a month apart. Since he had no other family, he was placed in an orphanage in the large city of Glasgow, Scotland. There, while still underage, he was forced into labor in a steel factory. The work was hard, and he was not treated well. The factory was hot and dark. He worked long hours, which returning to the orphanage every evening. The food at the orphanage was meager and tasteless, and Angus was continuously hungry. The other orphans weren't faring much better. It wasn't uncommon to hear crying and whimpering at night in the large dormitory. Angus felt that life was unrelievedly miserable and severe. Glasgow was an industrial city blanketed by thick smog from the local factories that frequently caused caustic irritation to the eyes and lungs. There was a pervasive smell of garbage and manure since sewage removal systems were rudimentary and all transportation was via animals. Because of the poor environmental conditions, disease and illness of all types were common. This urban environment was a stark contrast to the beautiful highlands covered with flowering purple heather and crisp, clean air. Angus's parents had been hardworking people who'd given him unconditional love, education, and plenty to eat. Now all that was gone.

After a year in the orphanage and working in the steel factory, he ran away and hitched a ride on a steamship to Canada. His passage was granted by the goodwill of the boat's captain, who felt sorry for the young waif. He did odd jobs for a while in Toronto until he finally landed a job at the Hudson Bay Company. His initial job was tanning furs and then taking inventory in a huge warehouse, where he learned managerial and other business skills. He naturally gravitated to the rugged and independent trappers who brought in the furs from the sparsely populated Canadian wilderness. This was where he met Isha's father. Angus and Isha's father became partners as young men. Angus didn't like living in the congested city and had an affinity for the solitude of the wilderness. His trapping and hunting career with Isha's father led him deeper and deeper into the bush, where few white men had been.

After many long years Angus had become a wise old man with extensive experience of the wilderness. Everyone in the village liked and respected him. He was an asset to the village since he brought so many new and useful things to the people from the white world. He was also the village "medicine man" since he had access to the white world's medicines and ways of treatment. He had lengthy experience dealing with injuries and illnesses of all types. Angus combined the medical knowledge of the white world with traditional Native medicine to treat people. Because of the benefits he brought to the tribe and his likable good nature, he was honored by becoming one of the decision-making elders of the tribe despite his race.

Angus had a good relationship with his Cree clients and was generous with his customers regarding credit when needed. His log cabin served as his residence, general store, first-aid station, trade center, and meeting place. It was by far the largest and most sturdily built cabin in the area. The logs were twice the size of those used in the regular village cabins. Each log was locked tightly in place by large notches at each end. The cabin was built to last a lifetime. There was always a good fire going in the large stone fireplace, and the trading-post cabin was always warmer than other cabins. Hot coffee and tea were always brewing, a welcome luxury for the villagers. The cabin had wooden floors, which was uncommon in the village, as the majority of the cabins had dirt floors covered with pine and spruce boughs that were replaced every two to three weeks. The trading-post cabin had tables and chairs where many of the villagers liked to congregate and talk over a hot beverage served to them by Angus's wife while they smoked their pipes of tobacco.

Angus always aimed to please. The chief and village elders periodically met at the trading post. The warmth of Angus and his Cree wife made everyone feel at home. Outside the trading post was a large open-sided shed with long tables underneath a roof where portions of meat from the periodic communal hunts were distributed among the tribe. This was done by the chief and elders of the tribe. They divided the communal meat mostly among the infirm and elderly as well as families that didn't have male hunters. It was rare for anyone in the village to go hungry.

Isha walked into the trading post with Atu. He had to push firmly to open the sturdy log door. As he entered, he immediately felt the rush of comfortable warm air. The smells of coffee and sweet-smelling pipe tobacco permeated the cabin. He saw two men he knew drinking coffee and smoking their pipes at a table in the corner. They greeted Isha, and he waved in response. The two men looked at Atu with mild disdain but didn't show their inner thoughts out of respect for Isha. They continued their conversation in low tones with occasional chuckles while Isha conducted business with Angus.

"Well, hello, Isha, how have you been? I see you brought a friend with you today," the old man said in a thick Scottish brogue. Angus walked around the counter, smiling, knelt, and started rubbing Atu's head. The two men in the corner looked at Angus petting the dog, thinking it was a silly, childlike gesture. They wondered if treating dogs like friends was a white man's custom that Isha had picked up from Angus. However, their thoughts were fleeting, and they continued with their conversation and smoking their pipes. Isha could tell that Atu enjoyed the head rub and the attention. Long ago Angus had had his own dog-sled team and had taught Isha many aspects of dog training. Angus had great respect for his younger friend's abilities as a trapper and hunter and was happy that Isha had grown to become a respected member of the community. He had always pulled for him as a young boy, since Isha had been so close to his father and uncle. Isha told Angus that he planned to extend his trapline to one hundred miles.

Isha said in his rudimentary English, "I need a good wool shirt and long underwear. I have heard wool is very warm."

"Well, I think we can handle that. Yes, wool is very warm in cold weather, and it's light." Angus got up and walked around the counter. He reached up high on a shelf and brought out a thick red-and-black-checked wool shirt as well as undergarments.

Isha tried the shirt on, pulled the collar up next to his neck, and said, "The shirt is thick. I like the color red too, like your hat."

"You can have the shirt but not my hat. It's the only thing I have that's from the land of my birth."

"I would never take your hat! That is your totem, something that gives your spirit power. It is who you are; I understand this."

Angus smiled and nodded. Isha's remark showed Angus that he had insight into human subtleties as well as good manners. However, he'd always known Isha was a bright young man.

Isha continued, "From what animal is wool?"

"It's the hair from sheep. They cut off the hair twice a year and sell it; that's what we call wool. They raise many sheep in my old country. In fact, my hat is made of wool."

"What are sheep? Are sheep tame like dogs?"

"Yes, they're quite mild-mannered, but they're not nearly as smart as dogs. In fact, they're quite dumb. People eat the meat as well. Sometimes I think people are not much different than sheep."

"Why do you say that?"

"In the white world there are thousands of people. They frequently will blindly follow bad leaders without thinking with their own minds, with terrible consequences."

Isha responded, "That is strange. If people don't think for themselves, they lose what makes them human."

"Yes, I know, Isha. When there are multitudes of people, they become lazy and are easily led. I guess in a way they become tame and follow their leaders like dumb sheep."

"I wish we could tame moose like sheep. Life would be easier."

"When an animal is tame, we call it domesticated."

"Dom-est-i-cated? I will remember that word, meaning 'tame animal.'"

"Yes, it's very good that you always like to learn new things, Isha."

"Learning new things is always good. I'll also need four boxes .30-caliber rifle shells, tin of coffee, and small pouch of tobacco."

Angus placed the items on the counter. "Will there be anything else, my friend?"

"Nope." Isha placed his money on the counter. This was the last of his family's money for the year until he brought in more furs from the upcoming trek north. He hoped the money he would obtain from the trek north would be sufficient for his family's needs for well over a year and possibly two years.

Isha began looking with interest at some of the other items of apparel Angus had on his shelf. He pointed to a red plaid wool scarf and asked Angus, "What's that?"

Angus turned around and took it off the shelf. "It's a wool scarf to keep your neck warm in the cold. It's the same red plaid of the Mc-

Donald clan as my hat. The pattern is an insignia from where I came from, northwest Scotland."

"It's beautiful, like your hat," said Isha.

"Here, it's yours."

"For me, free?"

"Sure; it will remind you of a far-off country where I come from."

Isha handled it like it was almost sacred. He looked at Angus as if he had given him a bag of gold.

"Thank you, Angus! You are a good friend. This scarf is special because it is a gift from the heart." As he spoke, he made a gesture in sign language that was even more meaningful than what he could express verbally. He placed his hand over his heart, making a circle, then made a spiral movement of his hand toward the sky and pointed to Angus. This meant that the gift was deeply heartfelt and was given by the great spirit that dwelled within the other man.

"I borrowed a lot of things from your father that I was never able to return, so it all comes around." Angus was pleased that Isha was about to embark on the longest trapline anyone in the village had attempted in years, but he didn't know where.

"Yes, it does. It does all come around. I understand this about life and about good people like you, Angus."

"So where are you going, my friend?"

"Up north, Seal River country."

Isha had some difficulty with his English and had to think about the words he wanted before he spoke. This created a slow and deliberate speech pattern. He used intermittent sign language, which Angus knew well. Angus knew about as much of the Cree language as Isha knew English. Thus, between them plus the sign language, they were able to communicate well.

Isha was one of the few Cree villagers who knew any English. His father had thought it important to teach him because he knew his son would have to deal with white society in the future and wanted him to be able to communicate with Angus. Whenever Isha and Angus met, they tried to speak in English, albeit slowly. Isha liked to practice his English, and it was enjoyable for Angus because he rarely got to speak his native tongue. It was one of the unique things about their relationship.

Angus replied, "That's a rugged area, I've never been to the Seal River country, but I'll bet there are a lot of furs to be had up there. I would've liked to go up there when I was a young man but never got around to it. If you're going there, you'll need to be well prepared."

Although Angus didn't show any emotion at the mention of the Seal River country, he'd always had a bad feeling about that territory. Isha's father had been killed on the Seal River after capsizing his canoe while shooting some rapids. His canoe had been heavily laden with a butchered moose he'd shot. When the canoe tipped, he likely hit his head on a rock and drowned. Isha's father had made plans to begin trapping the region in the winter prior to the accident. Angus also knew of a trapper who many years ago had vanished in that region and never returned. Most people avoided the area because of its "bad luck." However, its potential for harboring many furs was undeniable.

Early death among the villagers was not uncommon in the harsh and primitive environment of the Cree. Accidents were relatively frequent among young men. Infections and disease were common in the pre-antibiotic era, with minimal if any medical care in the remote subarctic. Any minor injury could develop into a life-threatening situation. Angus was always quite busy, not only with being a merchant but with his practice of medicine, as he was constantly being consulted for all manner of problems.

Isha nodded his head regarding the Seal River country having good potential for furs and turned to walk out the door with Atu and his packages.

"Good luck, Isha, and you too, Atu. I'll see you when you get back from the Seal River country, hopefully with a whole load of beautiful furs!"

Isha waved goodbye. The two men sitting at the table waved back, still puffing on their pipes. Mrs. McDonald walked to the two men sitting at the table to refill their cups with coffee. She waved and smiled at Isha as he walked out and said, "Say hello to Cici for me."

Isha looked back and said, "I will," and waved again.

After Isha left, one of the two men in the corner said, "Did you hear that? Isha is heading into the Seal River country."

The other man replied, "I hope he doesn't end up like his father. It was tough to lose a good man like that."

"Have you ever been up there?"

"Nope, never wanted to take chances. The world is dangerous enough without taking added risks in areas you don't know much about, especially with a lot of bad rumors about it."

Angus ambled over to the table. "Can I get anything more for you fellas?"

One of the men said, "No thanks, Angus; we were just a little concerned about Isha going up to the Seal River country."

"Yes, it concerns me too. Isha is a damn good man. He's got a lot to live for with a young child and one on the way. No one ever said he lacked courage."

"Nope, that's for sure. He's one of our best," one man said. "If anyone can be successful in the Seal River country, it'll be Isha. I've got confidence in him. But I'm glad it's not me going up in that spooky area."

Angus said, "Even so, I'm going to say a prayer for him before he goes."

As Isha and Atu walked back through the village to his cabin, they passed Aingan's house. Aingan was sitting out front.

"Hey, nephew, who do have with you?" Aingan, like most of the villagers, thought it strange for Isha to bring a dog with him.

"This is Atu, my new lead dog."

"Is he your new best friend?" Aingan said sarcastically.

"Yes, uncle, he's my new friend."

"Do you speak dog, or does he speak our language?" Again, Aingan spoke in a humorous, sarcastic tone. "Bowwow, bowwow! Ha, ha, ha."

Isha chuckled at his uncle's mild kidding.

"Yes, yes, uncle," he said as he waved, turned, and went on his way back to his cabin on the lake.

Isha entered the house with Atu. This was the first time he had brought Atu into his home. Cici was strongly opposed to this. It was unheard-of for sled dogs to be brought into one's home. She especially had concerns about their three-year-old toddler despite Isha's reassurances. As soon as Isha brought Atu into the one-room cabin, the toddler tried to tackle the huge dog, forcefully tugging on Atu's ears with no response from the dog except to lie down. Cici was amazed at the big dog's gentleness. She and her mother thought that a good husband and provider like Isha deserved a few eccentricities and accepted Atu as a family friend.

Atu soon became a fixture in the household. The toddler played with Atu like a big stuffed toy. Atu accepted Isha and Cici's "puppy" as the offspring of the alpha pair, as in wolf society. His response to the toddler's rough play was to lick the child's face and let him climb all over him. It was unusual for a half-wild sled dog to feel comfortable indoors, having spent his entire life outside. Most likely he felt as though he were in a comfortable den with his family group. He seemed to adapt to full domestication with ease because of his close attachment to Isha. Playing with Atu kept their young son occupied so that Cici didn't have to watch him as closely while she cleaned the cabin or prepared food. Atu became like an older gentle sibling to the young boy, who slept beside him at night in a comfortable curled ball. Cici now looked upon Atu as a friend and an asset to the family.

By the time of the first snow, the dogs were working as a cohesive unit. Isha was especially pleased with Atu. He was stronger than ever before and had put on a considerable amount of muscular weight over the year, as had the other dogs. Isha gave them large portions of high protein, which included fish and internal organs of moose and caribou. The dogs' muscles bulged like those of football players after lifting weights to prepare for a season of competition. All the dogs had grown and appeared both thicker and more compact.

Prior to the snow, some of the villagers told Angus about Isha's unheard-of practice of running his dogs on the grass field close to the village. Angus thought this was an outstanding idea. He wondered why nobody had thought of it before. It made perfect sense to build up the dogs' strength and endurance by having them pull a sled across a more difficult surface than snow. He thought, *That young man has a real head on his shoulders.*

Angus was curious about how Isha and his dogs were doing now that it was close to trapping season. He walked from the trading post with Aingan to visit Isha. After they greeted Cici and her young son, they were surprised to see Atu stroll out of the cabin. Atu stretched and yawned as if he had been awakened from sleep. Aingan was silent but thought, *What in the world is this dog doing in my nephew's cabin? Has he lost his mind?*

The old white man, Aingan, and Isha walked to the dog enclosure, with Atu closely following Isha. As they entered the enclosure, Aingan reflexively began to pick up a stick. Isha quickly turned to him and said, "You won't need that, uncle."

Aingan dropped the stick and looked at him quizzically. Aingan knew of Isha's plan to trap the Seal River country to the north. Aingan had grave reservations about this decision, especially since his brother had lost his life there.

Aingan asked, "Why do you want to risk your life to go up there, Isha? There's plenty of fur to be had around here."

Isha replied, "It's not any more dangerous than anywhere else we go. There's just a lot of silly superstitions about that area. It could make me a wealthy man with all the furs I bring back."

"Why do you have to always be so different from everyone else?" Aingan said.

"I don't know, uncle, maybe because I'm related to you."

"Ha ha ha ha," Aingan laughed, showing several absent teeth and a bent lip.

One thing Angus knew was dogs. He was an expert in their care and their training.

Angus remarked, "These are the finest specimens of a dog team I've ever seen." He rubbed the fur of several of the dogs. "They have a thick coat of fur, far better than most because you fed them so well. They'll be better able to withstand the cold because of this. This will cause less stress on them and keep them healthier in bad conditions." Angus stroked several of the dogs' bodies and said, "These are strong dogs. They've got a lot of muscle. They'll serve you well on a long trek, my friend."

Isha smiled, nodded, and replied, "Yes, I think so."

"The strength and power these dogs will deliver will be the same as a group twice their number. I can't say I've ever seen a healthier bunch of canines," Angus said.

"Canines?" Isha said.

"It's another word for dogs."

"Ah, yes, canines. The canines learned well. Watch this," Isha said.

He barked out a command: "Sit, stay." Isha, Angus, and Aingan then slowly walked around the entire enclosure while the dogs dutifully held their sitting position, closely watching every move Isha made. Isha then stopped and ordered, "Come." Like a group of obedient schoolchildren, the seven dogs rushed to Isha, rubbing against him and wagging their tails. "Lie down." The dogs immediately lay on their bellies. "Get up." The dogs responded to the command and crowded around Isha and Angus. Aingan stayed away from the exuberant dogs and pretended not to look at them. Nicimos and Jabweh were more excited than the others and jumped up on Isha. He rubbed their heads and told them to sit, which they responded to immediately, looking obediently up at him for the next command. The dogs all followed Isha's orders in unison, like a well-drilled platoon of soldiers.

Angus looked at Isha and said, "It appears you are well prepared, my friend. You have a dog team like no other." He slapped Isha on the back. "You've put a lot of work into this bunch. Your father would be proud of you."

Angus walked to Atu and knelt in front of the big dog. He began rubbing his head and stroking his body. "Of all the sled dogs I've ever seen, I think this big one is special." Atu looked at the old white man, happy to receive the attention.

Isha answered in Cree so Aingan could understand: "I think so too. He's come far in the last year. He feels like a little brother to me."

Aingan rolled his eyes and said, "Little brother! A dog!" He was quite close to the other two men, but he thought calling a dog a little brother was a bit much. However, he couldn't help but be impressed with the healthy appearance of the dogs as well as their amazing obedience.

"Why don't you just kiss the dog?" Aingan said sarcastically.

Isha laughed while Angus smiled and stood up. Atu was still looking at the old man, begging for more attention.

"I've got to admit, these dogs do have a lot of meat on them. They're quite stout. They look like small bull moose with short legs and no antlers," said Aingan. He thought, *Isha is going to need a strong dog team to venture into an area like the Seal River country.* His brother had been killed even though he had been a highly experienced and skilled woodsman who'd spent his entire life in the bush. He had taught Isha the ways of the wilderness. He thought one of the best things his brother had left behind for Isha was a good reputation, which he knew Isha always tried to live up to.

Isha wanted the team to be in top condition for the approaching hundred-mile trek. He knew that his well-being depended in large part on the dogs. Although he knew the dogs were ready for the trek and rigors of the subarctic winter, it was always good to have a little reassurance from his knowledgeable old friend Angus and uncle Aingan.

Atu responded rapidly to commands and was at the peak of his ability. Isha thought Atu was the best lead dog he had ever seen. However, he was yet to be truly tested by the rigors of a long-distance trek in the frigid winter. They had no idea of the test that was in store for them.

The Tribal Caribou Hunt

By late fall snow was covering the land. Aside from a thin layer of ice at the shoreline, it was not yet cold enough to freeze the lakes solid. This was the time when caribou herds grazing on the flat plains of the northern tundra, rich in vegetation, began to migrate south to the vast forest regions. Instinct had imprinted them with the need to move to the forest to avoid the extreme cold and winter wind of the tundra. They would first gather in small groups and then slowly coalesce into large herds as they approached their age-old migration routes farther south, close to the Cree village.

Everyone was preparing for the annual caribou hunt, an exciting time in the village that they looked forward to all year. A successful hunt would supply the entire village with meat for the year. Nearly the entire tribe participated. The only people left behind were mothers with small children and people of advanced age who couldn't travel. Angus and his wife stayed in the village so that the trading post and other services were available to the people left behind and newcomers from more remote villages.

Cici desperately wanted to go on the hunt with her husband. She remembered many good times when she and her family had participated in the annual hunt. However, she knew her primary responsibility now was to care for her three-year-old son and her unborn baby.

Isha was eager to go since it would be the first real test of his dog team's capabilities prior to his one-hundred-mile solo trapping trek to the Seal River country. He was anxious to see how his dog team would compare to the others.

All the able-bodied adults, teenagers, and older children traveled to an area roughly thirty miles to the west where a long ravine created a natural bottleneck between two large, rocky hills. An expansive grassland area made a perfect migration zone above the ravine for many miles, heading south to the ravine. It formed a natural conduit for caribou herds to migrate along and graze as they went. The caribou would eventually have to go through the ravine between the two rocky hills, which was a natural ambush site prior to a river crossing. The tribe would station themselves with their weapons on top of both hills to shoot down at the caribou when they entered the ravine. They had taken advantage of this location for hundreds of years.

The tribe traveled close to the ambush site and set up a temporary camp. Shelters in the form of tepees were set up along with a communal cooking area. The people carried their equipment in backpacks and dog sleds. Travois were placed on individual dogs to carry items as well. There was a social hierarchy among dogs in the village, as with humans. The dogs carrying the travois were usually not as fast or not as good at following commands as the sled dogs. They tended to be a little past their prime as well. The sled dogs had the ancient and distinctive honor of running with the hunt.

After setting up camp, the people traveled to the hills overlooking the ambush site. The caribou had yet to arrive. They lay in wait, ready to shoot down at the caribou with their rifles and muskets. A few of the older men and boys still used bows and arrows. There was no way of telling when nature would compel the herds to move. Some years the people could wait as long as several weeks if the herds were slow. To miss the caribou migration would place a great hardship on the tribe. The hunt was a great preventer of famine, especially for the weak and elderly. While waiting in the camp, the people felt constant vigilance and low-level anxiety. The chief, who managed the hunt, sent scouts out daily to determine the location of the herd.

After several days of anxious waiting on the hills above the canyon, the chief and the elders decided to send the men with dog sleds out as a group. The plan was for them to travel farther west to find the caribou and drive them toward the ambush site, where the villagers would be ready for them. They broke into two groups of four dog-sled teams, hoping the groups would be on either side of the herd. Most teams had ten to fourteen dogs, as opposed to Isha's seven. All the dogs were excited to start since they instinctively sensed the upcoming hunt from the preparations of their masters. Running with the hunt was something they were genetically programmed to do by their original wolf-like ancestry. Soskin's team was next to Isha's. Atu looked over at Soskin's lead dog, Lolo, with his one floppy ear. Upon catching Atu's gaze, Lolo immediately lowered his head and looked away.

The sled dogs and hunters set out on the quest to find and drive their prey toward the ravine. Isha's team bolted out fast and easily maintained a blistering pace. Soskin was close behind Isha but even with twelve dogs was straining to keep the pace set by Isha's team. He had sold Atu and the other dogs to Isha and couldn't believe his eyes. The dogs seemed like different animals from when he had sold them. They were nearly twice their original size and running like the wind without expending much effort. He was shocked that Atu, whom he had thought of as timid and without the ability to lead, was now heading the most impressive dog team he had ever seen.

Luck was with the hunters. To their surprise, within forty minutes they found the beginning of the caribou herd. They stationed themselves along the stretched-out herd while Isha and several other teams raced to the back of the herd so that they could turn the caribou and stampede them through the gauntlet of hunters with their stationary sleds and then toward the ravine and the main ambush site.

Isha called out to his team, "MUSH, MUSH, YAW!," telling the dogs to run at maximum speed. The dogs bolted to a new level of speed, and the abrupt change in velocity nearly knocked Isha's head back. Isha lowered his head and looked back at Soskin and his team. They were now far behind. Soskin was yelling obscenities at his dogs and cracking his whip in a futile attempt to gain speed. Lolo and Soskin's other dogs were already giving their best effort. They were running disjointedly, not as a confluent team. Their tongues were hanging out as they tried to breathe more air, and they were obviously beginning to tire.

Suddenly one of the hunter lost control of his dog team. They turned in front of the herd, running straight at the caribou, giving in to their natural tendency to run at and attack their prey instead of staying at the edges of the herd. This completely disrupted the plan to envelop the caribou and drive them toward the ambush site. The dogs obviously lacked the discipline and training of the other teams. The hunter struggled unsuccessfully to turn his dogs back to the side. When the caribou saw the errant dog sled coming straight at them, they abruptly turned and began running away from the ambush site. Isha and the others knew that if the caribou continued in the direction they were heading, they would scatter and find another place to cross the river. This would deprive the village of its much-needed meat, resulting in great hunger and hardship.

Isha knew he had to outrace the herd and then turn it back toward the ambush site. The other dog teams were now far behind, with the caribou herd ahead of them. Isha looked back one last time and noted that Soskin's dogs were now at a trot, while his team was continuing its all-out sprint with no sign of tiring. The caribou had outpaced the other dog teams, but not Isha's. He slowly caught up to the stampeding herd and stayed alongside it. He was now the only one who could turn the herd and thus stave off disaster.

"MUSH, MUSH, MUSH, YAW, YAW!" It was a race between the thundering hundreds of caribou and Isha's dog team. Isha could hear the heavy breathing and pounding of the herd's hooves just yards away from his side. He could see the crystallizing vapor from the caribous' rapid breathing in the cold air, giving the impression of dragons expelling smoke from their nostrils. The noise of the panicked herd was deafening. The dogs sensed fear in the caribou, which further stimulated their instinct for the chase, but they remained disciplined under Isha's commands and stayed to the side of the herd. Isha's dog team was slowly gaining, passing one caribou at a time. They were finally within a few yards of the lead animal, a large bull.

The team was in a full-out sprint, the fastest they had ever run by far. They were running at a different level, transformed into something Isha had never witnessed before. Isha barely recognized them. They dogs were running at a gallop in unison, following every muscular stride of their leader, Atu. Isha saw the back muscles of the dogs rippling as a wave together, like one large animal. Their heads were pointing straight ahead with their ears down, indicating maximum speed. The paws of each dog hit the snowy ground at the same time. This was perfection. They were in total harmony as one mind and one body. This was something that couldn't be taught by any sled-dog master, including Isha. This was what they were made to do by ancient instinct: to chase their intended prey and follow the alpha leader of the pack muscular move by muscular move. The three fastest dogs at the front, Atu, Jabweh, and Nicimos, were setting the pace for the other four. Isha felt exhilarated, as if his body were flying with the wind. He began to worry about abruptly stopping the team at such a speed for fear of a dangerous crash, but he put that fear out of his mind.

The dog team sped nearly seventy yards past the large bull and turned in front of the herd. "HO!" The dogs stopped immediately. The herd was rapidly approaching Isha. If the stampeding caribou didn't stop or turn, he and the dogs would be trampled to death, but Isha couldn't think about that now. He rapidly removed his mittens and grabbed his lever-action rifle. He jumped off the sled and fired several shots in the air, then waved his arms while yelling at the top of his voice. The entire herd stopped and made a quick about-face, back to where the villagers were waiting in ambush. Isha commanded the dogs to lie down.

All but one caribou retreated. The large bull that was leading the herd in retreat stopped and faced Isha. He had majestically large antlers sticking up in the air like a huge, dangerous, outlandish crown. This was one of the largest and healthiest caribou Isha had ever seen, and he had never seen a solitary caribou stand its ground in the face of a man. They were usually fearful animals that ran away from the slightest sign of danger. For a fleeting moment, Isha and the bull looked at each other. The bull knew what he had to do to protect his herd. He was not going to retreat like the others. He lowered his huge head with his spear-like antlers and pawed the ground as a sign of aggression. Isha recognized the bull's intentions and cocked his lever-action rifle, placing another cartridge in the barrel. The clicking sound of the rifle engaging stimulated the bull into full attack fury.

The bull launched toward Isha like an explosive cannonball. Isha quickly brought his rifle up to his shoulder and aimed at the caribou's head. This was not a good angle from which to shoot the charging beast. The optimal shot would be to the heart if the animal showed its side, but this was not to be. The head was bobbing up and down as the animal charged, making a good shot difficult. Isha carefully took aim at the moving target and fired. The bullet knocked off one of the two large antlers at its base. The bull, undeterred, kept charging without losing a step. Isha recocked the rifle and fired a second shot, which glanced off the bull's skull, causing only superficial damage.

The bull was closing fast. Isha had only one more chance before he was impaled by the bull's remaining antler and then trampled. The bull was further enraged by his nonfatal injuries and increased the speed of his charge to kill this man attacking his herd. Isha took a deep breath, slowly exhaled, and then fired. The bullet hit the bull between the eyes, deeply penetrating its brain. The bull fell headlong into the snow and slid several yards, coming to rest at Isha's feet. Isha breathed a long sigh of relief.

The rest of the hunters and dog teams were finally catching up with Isha. Several hundred yards away, another hunter with his dog sled had just arrived and had witnessed the whole event with the charging bull. He raised his rifle in the air, pumped it up and down several times, and let out an ancient Cree war cry, honoring the bravery of both man and beast.

Isha knelt next to the fallen bull and placed his hand on the courageous animal. He prayed to the Great Spirit and to the spirit of the bull. Isha felt that such a brave animal should be respected for his gallantry and his willingness to give his life to protect his herd. The other hunter yelled at Isha, "Let's go! What are you waiting for?" He then turned his sled around and followed the back of the herd, pushing them along toward the ambush site with the other hunters and dog teams.

Isha slowly walked to his sled, yelled "MUSH," and headed toward the retreating herd. He would return later to butcher the fallen bull. Without the extraordinary efforts of Isha and his dogs, the hunt would have been unsuccessful and the people would have gone hungry. Isha felt relieved and proud of his team, especially Atu.

While Isha was following the herd, he glimpsed something moving silently in the forest. He quickly looked to the side. Only thirty yards away, moving in and out of his peripheral vision through the trees like phantoms, was a wolf pack. The wolves had been stalking the caribou during their migration, picking off any stragglers that were weak, sick, injured, or old. Any carcasses the humans left behind would be theirs.

Isha thought fleetingly that they were hunters like him, following the caribou just as he and his tribe were. He stopped for a moment to look at the wolves. The other hunters with their dog sleds were gone, chasing the caribou back to the ambush site. There was no need for him to follow quickly. He had already done his job. Isha noted that the wolves stopped as a huddled group and stared at him, seemingly curious about another hunter. He counted seven individuals. They showed no fear or aggression, just curiosity. He was alone with the wolves. Isha waved and gave a short howl with his hands cupped around his mouth. Instead of fleeing into the forest, the wolves continued to stare at him with an unusual silent intensity. Wolves usually run away at the sight of men. Isha had seen many wolves before, but only in fleeting glimpses. He knew they were always nearby, but they naturally stayed away from humans.

There seemed to be something more to this event than met the eye. The way they all stared at him in such curious depth, as if they were trying to communicate something, he had never seen before in animals, though he had experienced a similar sensation when he had first seen Atu in Soskin's pen. Isha wondered if this was an omen from the Great Spirit. The nonverbal connection between the two hunters was broken when he finally called out to his dogs and went on his way, chasing the herd. Isha looked back to see that the wolves were still stationary, looking at him.

After traveling nearly a mile, Isha had the strange sensation that he was being watched. He turned and to his shock saw the wolf pack loping casually toward him, about eighty yards away. There was no reason for them to follow him. He was not carrying food. If anything, they should have headed for the downed bull caribou. Unusual or not, Isha was not about to take a chance with a group of potentially dangerous animals coming at him, albeit relatively slowly. He stopped the sled, removed his mittens, and grabbed his rifle. When he turned to aim, to his astonishment, the wolves were gone as if they had evaporated into thin air! He brought his rifle down and stood scanning the area. He neither saw nor heard anything. He thought, *They probably turned around to get the caribou carcass. But how could they go out of sight so quickly?* Isha turned his sled around and headed back to get the caribou bull before the wolves could.

On his way, he saw the wolf tracks in the snow. He stopped to quickly investigate. The tracks simply stopped. The wolves had either vanished into thin air or abruptly turned in the opposite direction and fled rapidly, following their original trail. He was perplexed. *Why would they do that? Why not run to the nearest edge of the forest, which was much closer? Why backtrack the way they came? To be gone so quickly, within a minute, while I was getting my gun, they must have run incredibly fast. I think it was impossible to turn and run out of my sight within that short a time. I know I'm not imagining this because I see their tracks.*

Isha jumped back on the sled and drove to the bull. He found the downed animal exactly as he had left it. There was no sign of the wolves. He field dressed the bull, taking the meat and the hide and placing it in the sled. After he finished, he again silently scanned the area and found no sign of wolves. He shook his head in disbelief, jumped back on the sled, and proceeded to the ambush site.

Within minutes Isha heard the resounding sound of extensive gunfire in the distance. He knew the caribou herd had entered the ambush site. Men of all ages were firing from the hills on both sides at the animals below. As the animals were shot, their fallen carcasses caused the others to trip and fall over them, creating easier shots for the hunters. Some of the caribou tried to turn in the opposite direction to flee the ambush, only to run into the onrush of the stampeding herd, creating more confusion and havoc. Chaos and panic were everywhere within the confines of the ravine. The explosive noise of gunfire from the tribe and the bellowing and screaming of frightened, dying animals could be heard for miles around. Several men were stationed at the riverside to shoot the caribou that were lucky enough to pass through the ravine as they jumped into the water. This made them easy targets for the men on the shore only a few yards away. The river became a river of death, choked with dead, floating caribou from shore to shore. The men would later retrieve the animals by canoe and drag them to the riverbank.

It was one of the most successful caribou hunts that anyone could remember. The tribe was jubilant at their success. Over one hundred animals were killed. Men, teenagers, and women, young and old, flooded down the steep, rocky hills like throngs of hungry vultures to butcher the animals. It didn't take long to field dress the caribou. The meat was placed in backpacks and on the dog sleds, each of which was piled high with meat and hides. The tribe went back to their temporary camp and had a communal feast that evening. They built a large bonfire in the middle of the camp, and the flames rose high and illuminated the entire area. All gathered around the giant fire, which gave off great warmth in the cold late-autumn night. It was a joyous party atmosphere as they celebrated the great victory. All danced, sang, and feasted that night, as they had done for hundreds and possibly thousands of years. This was a special time of rejoicing and communal bonding.

Aingan and Soskin approached Isha at the bonfire, both smiling. Everyone knew about Isha's heroic deed of turning the herd around toward the ambush when the caribou were on the verge of scattering in the opposite direction. Aingan was carrying an entire cooked front leg of a caribou, hoof and all. He held it with both arms as he would carry a child. It was larger than a human leg. He appeared to be feasting on a giant prehistoric drumstick, which seemed to fit his personality. Between swallows of meat, he slapped Isha on the back and said, "You did well today, nephew. You have trained your dogs well. Your father would be proud of you."

Soskin said, "What did you do to those dogs, especially Atu? They're different animals. I'm not even sure they're dogs anymore. I didn't recognize them. They're more like wolves. Did you change them by magic?"

Isha and Aingan laughed.

"Yes, a bit of magic," Isha said, waving his arms around as if creating a spell.

"I couldn't keep up with you at all, and I had my best twelve dogs. Your dogs aren't normal!" said Soskin.

The three men laughed again as they feasted on their well-deserved caribou dinner. Isha mentioned his experience with the wolf pack during the hunt. He also told them of his dream of being attacked by wolves over a year ago. Soskin's and Aingan's demeanor suddenly changed. They fell silent and stared seriously at Isha.

Soskin broke the silence and said, "The old ones in the village would call that a sign or an omen. I don't know if I believe in that or not, but it certainly is an experience that shouldn't be discounted. Just to be safe, I would seek guidance from the Great Spirit as to the meaning of this and what you should do."

"Aahh, that's a bunch of superstitious rubbish. If you live long enough in the bush, you're always going to see something strange," Aingan said as he munched on his caribou leg.

Soskin changed the subject and grinned as he looked at Aingan. "What are you going to do with the rest of that big piece of meat?"

"I'm taking it to bed with me so I can gnaw on it during the night and when I wake up tomorrow."

"Only animals sleep with their food, like bears or wolves. Humans don't do that! After the meat is gone, are you going to gnaw on the hoof?" said Soskin.

All three men laughed.

"You should know by now that Aingan is more animal than human," said Isha.

"I feel sorry for your wife. She must have her hands full living with a beast like you!" Soskin responded.

Aingan raised the caribou leg over his head and growled. All three men laughed loudly. Isha went into his shelter for the night, fully satisfied after a roasted caribou dinner. He lit his pipe and relaxed, watching the small cloud of smoke rising to the top of the shelter. It had been a good day. He was satisfied that he had done his duty and that the tribe would be well fed for over a year. He was also pleased with the dogs' performance. He had known they were good, but they had showed him that they were capable of another level of ability that he hadn't expected. He put his pipe down and slowly drifted into a deep sleep.

That night he had a vivid dream in which a giant wolf stepped out from behind a huge black rock with a flat surface. For some reason Isha felt that the black rock had some deep significance, almost like something sacred that he couldn't define. The giant wolf slowly approached without aggression, only curiosity, like the wolves he had seen the day before. Isha had no fear of the wolf. He was as curious about the wolf as the wolf was about him. The giant wolf was between Isha and the black rock, not allowing Isha to get closer, even though Isha felt drawn to the rock. They were just a few yards away from each other when Atu walked between them. Atu was perfectly calm but tried to lead Isha away from the wolf, as if Atu could communicate with him without speaking. That was when he woke up.

He abruptly sat up, rubbing his face with his hands and taking a deep breath. "What do these dreams mean? What is this strange black rock I've never seen before?" Isha felt confused, as if the Great Spirit were talking to him in a language that he didn't understand. He shook his head and slapped his cheeks to fully awaken himself from the vivid dream.

He got up and walked outside his shelter in the cold, crisp night air of late autumn. A heavy mist wafted above the snow-covered ground. The sun had yet to rise above the horizon. The camp was silent, still sleeping after the big festivities the night before. Isha left the camp alone, walking about a mile to the top of a small hill. He knelt and looked up at the gray early-morning sky.

He raised his arms and said, "What are you trying to tell me, Great Spirit? What is it you want me to do? Give me the wisdom to understand what you are trying to tell me. Do these dreams and signs mean anything? Do they have something to do with my trip to the Seal River country?"

Isha realized that there were too many signs about wolves to be merely coincidences. He felt confused. He had the sensation of being a pawn in some complicated spiritual game in which he had no idea of the rules or the outcome. He put his head in the snow and yelled in frustration. As he raised his head, the sun slowly crept above the horizon. He observed the golden rays piercing the sky in silence for some time, as if waiting to be spoken to. He finally arose, disappointed, and went back to camp, still in a spiritual quandary.

Upon returning to camp, Isha hooked the dogs to the sled. The people were starting to rise and fix breakfast, after which they headed back to the village on Lake Kashapon. Isha's sled was piled high with meat and hides. It looked like a small mountain and weighed over three hundred pounds. The other hunters couldn't believe their eyes when they saw Isha's dogs pulling such a heavy load with relative ease.

The caravan of villagers carried the spoils of victory in a long line, slowly walking back to the village, where the hides, meat, and other parts of the caribou were distributed in the large open-air shed next to Angus McDonald's trading post.

Isha was proud of his dogs. Atu and the rest of the team seemed to know they had performed well. They were exuberant, and they licked and brushed up against one another, wagging their tails high in the air while Isha rubbed their heads and gave them treats of dried fish. Isha was now confident that his dog team was ready for the Seal River country and any hardship that might face him. Little did he know that he would face something greater than he had ever known existed.

Prelude to the Trek

Isha had to wait for the lakes to freeze solid before going to the Seal River country. This gave him a little time to consider the signs he had seen and the dreams he was having. He told Cici about his most recent dream and his experience with the wolves on the hunt, but she didn't know what to think. She said, "Why don't you talk to Angus about this and see what he thinks? You might even talk to Tiskigapon."

The Cree tribe had been converted to Catholicism by Jesuit missionaries many years before; however, most villagers still believed in spirits as well. Angus was the closest thing the village had to a Christian missionary. People knew he was very devout and knew a lot about the Bible, "the black book of all knowledge," although he didn't profess to be of any specific religious denomination. He was also widely recognized for his wisdom and good nature. It helped greatly that he was easy to talk to, mixing good advice and biblical teachings with frequent humor.

Tiskigapon, on the other hand, was an elderly woman in her nineties who lived alone in a small cabin close to Angus's trading post. She was quite healthy for someone of such an advanced age and still had an active and inquisitive mind. She was reportedly close to the spirit world, although she professed Christianity as well. She was a member of the Midewiwin, or what some people called a shaman. She knew traditional Native medicine and supposedly had the ability to heal minor problems with potions, medicinal plants, and spiritual intervention. Angus had learned the ways of traditional Native medicine from her. They were friends and had great respect for one another. She knew the history and myths of the tribe and would tell stories that everyone loved, especially the children. Isha fondly remembered listening to Tiskigapon's tales when he was a boy.

To the villagers, Angus represented the changing new world of technology and Christianity, whereas Tiskigapon represented the old ways and the spirit world. Both were respected by the people, who felt that both had a place in their lives.

Isha went to the trading post to see Angus. He walked in and saw Angus sitting at a table.

"Well, hello, Isha, what can I do for you? Do need some more items for the big trek north?"

"No, I need some advice."

"Well, have a seat and we can talk." Angus could tell as soon as Isha walked through the door that Isha was not his usual smiling, happy self. He immediately detected that something was weighing heavy on Isha's mind.

Isha sat down, placed his hands together on the table, and leaned toward Angus, looking at him sincerely. He told Angus of his recurring dreams and how he had seen the wolf pack during the hunt. Angus was not expecting such a question from his young friend. He had never been confronted with anything like this before.

Angus leaned back in his chair, stroked his beard, and said, "Oh, I see how this could give you great concern. According to the Bible, there have been many people who the Lord has spoken to, but he usually makes himself clear to the recipient of the dream. It may take time, but it usually becomes apparent. His time is not like our time, and his ways are not our ways."

"Do you think I may be in danger if I go on this trek to the north?"

"I don't know, Isha. I don't have the ability to interpret signs or dreams. I do know your father was always planning to go and trap the area."

"I know. I used to look on that region with great curiosity as a young boy when trapping with him. That place was always mysterious and seemed to beckon me."

Angus leaned over the table, looked Isha in the eyes, and said, "It's not really about the furs and the money is it, Isha?"

"I guess not, Angus. I think getting more money was an excuse to go into that region. It's something I've always wanted to do, for some strange reason. However, there's no doubt the area is a great prospect for furs, and I'm the last person to pass up some extra money for a little extra work. But you're right—there's something more. I just wish I had come to this conclusion before I was married and had children. Now I have so much to lose if things go terribly wrong."

Angus said, "The fear of the unknown is universal to everyone. I was afraid when I came alone to Canada as a young lad, not knowing what to expect in a different country. I was also afraid of going into the bush for the first time with your father. I went into the wilderness with no idea what it was like living and working there. I didn't even know the language of your people. Thank goodness I met your father who showed me how to live out here and speak Cree. It surely is a far cry from the Scottish Highlands. After those big steps in my life, here I am, happy as a clam. Sometimes the Great Spirit places a great challenge in front of a young man to make him into the man the Lord wants him to become. Sometimes it can be painful, and we don't understand it, but you must follow your heart or you'll feel incomplete, always wishing you had heeded the Great Spirit's challenge for you. It may be like forging a steel sword from rough iron by undergoing fire and pounding on an anvil." Angus paused briefly to reflect.

"Great leaders must always face painful challenges, but usually they win in the end. To venture into the unknown and conquer a great obstacle takes courage. The struggle to achieve the goal will give you insight and wisdom after it's done. It's what makes good leaders different than average people. You will see things differently than others because of the experience. These few people can sense things that are not outwardly apparent to others."

"You mean like seeing bear tracks going beyond a hill and hearing bushes move there, but you cannot see the bear, yet you know it's there?"

"Yes. It's like having the ability to see beyond the hill. Some people have the ability, but most don't. The ability to 'see beyond the hill' can be developed through surmounting a great challenge requiring courage and persistence. However, this path can be quite dangerous and painful. It is, however, the way of the warrior."

"Did my father have this ability to 'see beyond the hill'?"

"Oh yes, very much so. I feel strongly that you are heading for a leadership position in the tribe one day. I know you haven't thought about this, nor have we discussed it. However, your father and I talked of this frequently. You have great abilities that you are not aware of yet, my young friend. Prior to taking on a great challenge that you know might be dangerous, you must prepare yourself physically, mentally, and spiritually. You must seek the Great Spirit within you, for it is he who will give you strength beyond your natural abilities."

Angus continued, "You might talk to Tiskigapon and see what she says about your dreams. She's a smart and gifted woman. She also cares about the welfare of the tribe. However, you should take what she says with a grain of salt."

Isha said, "'Grain of salt,' what does this mean?"

"It means you can't believe everything you hear from her, but she may speak many truths as well."

"Yes, a grain of salt, I will remember this when I speak to her. You are very wise, Angus."

"Remember, once you make your decision, don't ever second-guess yourself. Otherwise you will lose confidence if something doesn't go as planned, and you will be less effective in your endeavor. Whatever you decide, I will always support you, no matter the outcome."

"Yes, I understand this, and I am grateful for your support," Isha said.

The two men got up from the table and shook hands. "Thank you, Angus, for being such a trusted friend."

"Come back anytime if you wish to talk again, my friend."

The following evening Isha went to Tiskigapon's small cabin on the outskirts of the village. He knocked on the wooden door. "Come in," came a muffled, squeaky voice from within the cabin.

Isha opened the door and had to duck because the doorway was so small. He entered the dimly lit one-room cabin, lowering his head so he wouldn't scrape the rafters. The cabin was warm and comfortable from the slowly burning orange embers in the fireplace. It was dimly lit by the amber hue of several tallow candles and the fireplace. The room had a beautiful aromatic smell of various medicinal herbs. Along the walls were wooden storage shelves where leather satchels containing herbs and medicines were stored.

"Well, Isha, I haven't seen you in many years! My, you have grown. You look a lot like your father. He was such a good man. Everyone misses him to this day. Have a seat."

"Thank you." He took off his hat and sat on a markedly undersized chair next to a small table. The chair was so tiny that his knees nearly touched his chest. He felt as if he were in a cabin built for a child with miniature furniture. The cabin felt like an immaculately clean, warm, and tidy cave.

"Would you like some Labrador tea? I made some this morning, and I have plenty."

"Sure, thank you."

The old woman was a tiny person to begin with but was now bent over from chronic arthritis, which had taken a toll on her body over the years. She moved slowly and deliberately. Her face was covered with deep furrows and wrinkles upon wrinkles, giving testimony to her ninety-two years. However, her eyes were clear and seemed to sparkle, indicating her mental acuity. Her happy omnipresent smile made Isha feel at ease in the cramped, dark little cabin. Tiskigapon poured some tea with her gnarled, trembling little hands into a wooden cup and gave it to Isha. She sat down on a tiny chair, which fit her body perfectly.

"Well, now, what can I do for you, young man?" she asked him with a smile, at the same time looking deeply into his eyes to detect meaning beyond his words. Isha told the old woman about the dreams and signs and where he intended to go.

Her voice was calm, but her eyes betrayed her unease. "Oh my! The area to the north where you are intending to go is an area of great danger. It has been that way for many, many years. Our tribe originated there long, long ago. A demon from the underworld called the Wendigo stalked the people of our tribe, killing everyone it could ambush, including children. It killed not only people but all creatures it could catch. It wanted death to all living things, but especially human beings. It was over fifteen feet tall and walked on two hooved legs. It had horns on its head and scales for skin. It had large teeth that were poisonous. It had large, bulging red eyes. It lurked around the edges of the village, where it would pounce on any unsuspecting person. This beast was made by the devil, the Great Evil Spirit. Many warriors from the tribe tried to kill the beast with spears and arrows, but they always failed. The Wendigo was too quick and clever to be killed by human beings alone. The hunters became the hunted as the Wendigo stalked anyone who ventured too far from the village. The people prayed to the Great Spirit and asked what they should do. They were told to seek assistance from the giant cave bear. The chief of the tribe along with several warriors went to the large cave where the giant bear lived. They asked him to please help them kill the Wendigo since it was killing all animals and the bear also would go hungry if the Wendigo was not killed.

"The great bear agreed to help rid the land of this monster, so they devised a plan. The people would serve as bait and run away from the Wendigo while the bear hid behind a large boulder and jumped on the Wendigo's back as it passed by, chasing the warriors. The plan worked perfectly. The giant bear leaped on the Wendigo's back and bit it in the neck, killing the Wendigo. However, with its last movement the monster bit the giant bear in the foot, poisoning the bear. The bear knew he was dying and walked to a beautiful place by a waterfall overlooking a huge lake, where he lay down and died. The people prayed to the Great Spirit to do something so they would remember the bravery of the bear. The Great Spirit listened to them and turned the giant bear into a large black rock after he died. The Great Spirit saw the good things that the giant black bear had done for the humans and therefore populated the world with smaller versions of the great bear so humans and bears could easily coexist.

"The black rock is still there and is sacred to our people. This is the reason we are the Bear Clan of the Cree tribe. We are the most honorable of all clans among the Cree nation. In the old days people from our tribe used to make pilgrimages to the black rock to receive power and inspiration. It is said that you receive its greatest power at dawn.

"By the time the Wendigo was killed, the land had already been depleted of all animal life from years of destruction, so there was no food to hunt. So the tribe moved south to Lake Kashapon, where we live now. Our clan used to have a sacred duty to care for and protect the area where the large black rock is, but time has eroded our responsibilities to the spirit world. When there is so much death and evil in a land, a negative force remains behind—except for the black rock, which stands as an isolated positive force. This land remains a dangerous and negative region. But one day it is destined to change for the positive."

"Positive and negative forces in the land, how can this be?" said Isha.

"Most places are neutral, but some special and unique areas in this world retain good or bad spirits from events that happened there. The spirits in the land may last for centuries or for who knows how long, but the negative spiritual force of a region can be changed by an overwhelming opposite force for the good."

"Have you ever seen this big black rock?" Isha said.

"No, but one day our tribe will return and turn a negative land into a strongly positive one, just as the Jews returned to the promised land."

Isha didn't know anything about the Jews or the promised land, so he let that go.

Tiskigapon went on, "I feel the wolves in your dream and especially the giant wolf may represent some kind of force keeping you and the tribe from our original land, since the giant wolf was in front of the black rock, keeping you away from it. The wolf seems to think it's his territory. He's certainly willing to kill to protect what he thinks is his land. It seems that the dog in your dream is a protective force since you were not killed as in your original dream a year ago. Quite possibly the dog was sent to you by the Great Spirit to protect you. If your dream a year ago was your only dream, I would suggest you not go to the north. However, now you and the giant wolf looking at each other without fear means you are equals with some level of respect. This I don't understand, but I'm sure you will comprehend it more clearly in the future. One thing you must try to avoid at all costs is making a wolf your adversary. They are too much like human beings. They are highly intelligent and work together in packs, as we do. If deeply angered, they can be a vicious and relentless enemy.

"There is certainly a risk to your life if you go to the north. I have great concern for you because I truly believe the dreams and signs you experienced are not trivial and emanate from the Great Spirit. However, you or one of your family may be the one to lead our people back to their sacred land and turn a negative region into a positive one. The Seal River country to the north operates by its own rules, and humans are mere visitors to this dangerous and lonely realm. There's more to this place than a man can ever see with his eyes, a lot more than he can ever hope to understand. One must always beware of trying to force one's will against fate. I hate to say this, Isha, but you may have too much to lose if you enter that evil region as your father did."

She abruptly changed her demeanor to a less serious one and said, "Would you like some more tea?" as she smiled across the tiny table. Isha was silent, deep in thought, trying to absorb all that had been said. This was far more information than he had expected and somewhat troubling.

"No, thank you, thank you very much for your help. I must be on my way," Isha said as he stood up, nearly hitting his head on the low rafters.

Isha had never heard the story of the Wendigo before, and he wasn't sure what to make of it or how it pertained to him. He decided to take Tiskigapon's story with a great amount of salt, as Angus had said.

It was dark as he walked back to his cabin. The village was dead silent, the only sounds his footsteps rhythmically crunching the packed, dry snow. He remained in deep thought about the trek north and his dreams. He considered what Angus and Tiskigapon had said. He thought about his father, Cici, and their children. He had put a tremendous amount of his time, money, and effort into preparing for this journey, and many people in the village knew about his plan to begin trapping the Seal River country to the north. To stop now would seem cowardly.

His mind was made up. Nothing would deter him from what he felt was his destiny, no matter the danger. He thought, *This is my fate ordained by the Great Spirit, and I will face whatever it is with courage because I am a Cree warrior!*

Several weeks later, the night before Isha was to depart, he had another vivid dream, so real that it awakened him from sleep. He suddenly sat up, awakening Cici.

"What's wrong, Isha, another dream?"

"Yes, it was very strange. It was a little different from the dream I had over a year ago that was so terrible. This time I was on the sled with the dogs, and I saw a huge fight between two wolf packs. It was a terribly violent affair that created a lot of frightening noise. It was vicious. Out of the many wolves fighting, a huge male wolf disengaged from the fight and came walking toward me. He was the same large wolf I previously dreamed about. He was so close to me that I could see his yellow eyes. The other wolves stopped fighting and disappeared. The large wolf was alone, and we just stared at each other for the longest time. Everything was silent. He didn't show any signs of aggression, nor was I afraid. We just stared at one another, and then he vanished. I then looked back at the dogs, and all were gone except Atu, whose face was a large red blur with no identifiable facial features. Then I woke up. I'm glad at least I didn't get killed this time.

"People have more problems with a charging bull moose or with bears than wolves. I heard a story of a man who broke his leg in the Seal River country and couldn't move who was eaten by wolves, but that was long ago and may have been just a rumor."

"Maybe you're going to have some interaction with the people of the Wolf Clan of our tribe. But they live so far away. Who knows? You need to get some sleep. You have a big day tomorrow," replied Cici.

Isha lay back down and stared at the rafters, wondering about his vivid dream and its possible meaning. He did feel that there was some truth in most dreams, but he decided not to think about it further because it wouldn't change what he was going to do. He slowly drifted back into a deep sleep.

The next morning he awakened before sunrise, excited to start on his new adventure, for which he'd been preparing for over a year. He turned the sled over and used a handful of moose fat to grease the runners. He loaded his sled with his equipment and supplies and fed the dogs a large meal, which would be their biggest meal for quite some time until they returned. Isha put the dogs in their harnesses and attached them to the sled. The dogs' eyes were fixed on Isha as they fidgeted in their harnesses, eager to start. They, especially Atu, seemed to sense that this was the big day for which they had trained for so long. Isha placed his rifle on top of the sled, just under the canvas covering, for easy access.

Isha was an excellent shot and had won several competitions in the village with his American-made Winchester lever-action .30-.30-caliber rifle. This rifle was the type his father had used, and Isha had fired it thousands of times since his youth. There were more powerful rifles that could shoot farther that many village hunters used, such as the British Enfield; however, he preferred the seven bullets that the Winchester carried to the five of the Enfield. Additionally, he didn't feel comfortable with the bolt action of the Enfield, which he thought interfered with the sighting if multiple rapid shots were required.

Cici came out of their cabin covered in a thick fur robe, carrying their young child. She kissed Isha and made the sign of the cross over his forehead with her finger.

Isha carried a "medicine pouch" around his neck, a small leather bag embroidered with colorful beads with a unique design. It was an ancient tradition that was still used by most Cree hunters event though they had been converted to Christianity. The pouch was thought to bring power and good luck. Within it was a small segment of his umbilical cord, which had been saved for him by his mother, like most Cree mothers. This was thought to be a relic of his previous connection to the spirit world and, as such, closer to the Great Spirit, who would protect him. There was a bear claw that would provide strength and endurance, especially since he was from the Bear Clan of the Cree tribe. There was also a fang of the wolverine that would impart fearless, savage ferocity. Small cuttings of his young son's and Cici's hair were placed last within the medicine pouch to reassure him of love and support him if his spirit became weak.

Isha gave his young son a present before he left. He had carved the likeness of a dog like Atu from a caribou antler. He said, "This is a baby Atu that will keep you company while Atu and I are gone. We both will see you in a few weeks." His son grabbed the handmade toy and smiled.

At the break of dawn, Isha stood by the lake next to his cabin. Cici told him to be careful. Isha kissed his young son and softly patted Cici's pregnant belly. He told her that he expected to be gone roughly two weeks, weather permitting.

Angus had awakened early and made the two-mile walk from the trading post to see him off. He patted Isha on the back and said, "Good luck, young man." Angus then placed his hand on Isha's head and said a prayer for his friend.

The dogs were silently alert with their ears raised. Their eyes were fixed on every movement Isha made, anxiously awaiting his command to begin their great adventure.

The temperature was around 5 degrees below zero Fahrenheit, with clear skies and no wind. It was a beautiful day by local standards. Isha hopped onto the sled and yelled, "MUSH!" The dogs took off, eager to run, abruptly jerking the sled onto the frozen lake. Isha felt a rush of exhilaration now that he had begun the greatest adventure of his life.

Trapping the North

The village where Isha lived was located on one end of Lake Kashapon, which was now frozen. The dogs pulled the sled effortlessly even though it was partially loaded with gear. They felt as though they were pulling a load of feathers. Isha began to sing. The dogs' ears perked up. The two most fun-loving dogs, Nicimos and Jabweh, briefly looked back at Isha and seemed to smile. Isha felt that if dogs could sing, they would be singing along with him. The dogs' legs were elevated high above the snow with each step, almost as if they were prancing like caribou. Their heads were held high as if anticipating a great adventure.

Isha traveled for approximately five miles to the end of the lake. He then guided the dog team onto land where there was a well-established trail. They traveled from the wide-open space of the frozen lake into a tunnel-like trail through the brush. This trail marked the beginning of Isha's old trapline, which he and his family had used for years. Isha began setting traps just off the trail. In the past he would have walked this trail with snowshoes, taking an entire day to reach the end. Now, with the dog team, it took a mere two hours.

As he emerged from the confines of the sheltered trail into the open, the Seal River country lay before him. He could feel a palpable presence as he gazed upon the territory. It was such a vast expanse that it nearly took his breath away. Even the wind seemed to avoid this place as if respecting some unseen boundary. A dense frozen mist lay low over the huge lake. Within the mist, minute particles of water had crystallized in the cold, making the air sparkle yet seeming like an impenetrable shiny wall. As he silently looked at the lake, he could hear a slight high-pitched metallic tinkling sound, as if the entire world were sounding some subtle, barely audible alarm. The millions of tiny ice crystals in the strange mist were colliding with each other to make a sound that reverberated throughout the place. Isha considered this unusual occurrence an ominous harbinger of a dark revelation, telling him to turn back. He thought of the Seal River country as an adversary that needed to be vanquished in retribution for his father's death. He reminded himself that he was a brave Cree warrior and would not be deterred by fear. He had the feeling that after today everything in his life would be different.

"MUSH!" he yelled, and the sled took off past the large boulder and down the small ravine leading to the vast frozen lake, the entrance to the Seal River country.

He was quickly enveloped by the thick crystalline mist, which seemed foreboding as he drove his sled through it. It was like passing through a thick gray soup with sparkles all around him and the tiny ice particles lightly stinging his face. Although he couldn't see beyond his dog team, he continued on because he knew nothing was in front of him except a vast expanse of frozen lake. He had the sensation of being sucked into a strange world, as if being swallowed by a huge creature. He remembered what Tiskigapon had said about a negative energy to this place, and he was beginning to feel its heavy presence.

After several hours the mist burned away with the rising sun, and he could see the landscape more clearly. There was a stark change in the topography. The banks of the frozen lake were steeper here, with cabin-sized jagged boulders. The trees were taller, interspersed with large open areas of bare rock as well as patches of frozen swamp. This lake was vastly larger than Lake Kashapon. It appeared endless and enormously wide.

He had a brief sense of anxiety as he travelled, observing the land he had been so mystified by for so many years. However, this concern was quickly dissipated by his feelings of excitement and adventure.

As Isha traveled along the frozen waterway, he was surrounded by a deathly silence. On first sight this wilderness appeared devoid of animal life. Everything appeared frozen, with no sound or movement. All life requires great effort to survive in the frozen north. This severe world seems to want to kill everything slowly and inexorably, both predator and prey, but life refuses to die. Isha knew there were unseen animals surviving in their own way in this unforgiving environment.

The frozen lake was open and easy to navigate with the sled. Isha didn't have to contend with low-hanging branches, occasional fallen trees, hills, valleys, frozen streams, and other obstacles frequently found on trails through the bush. While following the shoreline of the frozen lake, he set traps and snares just off the banks of the frozen water. He marked the traps with a red cloth tied to a nearby tree branch so he could easily find them on his return. The routine of setting the traps distracted him from obsessing about the omnipresent foreboding feeling of this new environment.

At the end of the short northern day, the light of the sun became pale as it began to dip below the horizon. Isha stopped to make camp for the night. He built a small shelter of wooden poles in the form of a tepee. The structures he built were made for a single individual, measuring approximately ten by ten feet. He lashed the poles together with rope and placed moss between them for insulation. He then placed a large canvas over the structure. He laid spruce and pine boughs on the floor and spread a blanket over them, making a soft area off the cold ground to lie on. The shelter was comfortable and had the fresh scent of evergreen. In the middle he built a small fireplace with stones placed in a circle. The shelter offered effective protection from the freezing cold night.

He cut more pine boughs and placed them under a protective spruce tree after removing the snow for the dogs. The dogs huddled together as a group, forming one large ball of fur under the tree to conserve heat. Isha would construct several of these shelters along the entire length of the trapline. They would be anticipated campsites where he could rest after traveling a full day on his return.

Isha was hoping to shoot some game to help feed his dogs and not waste the meager rations he had brought for himself. For now, however, he was going to settle down for the night. He fed the dogs some frozen fish and pemmican and then entered his shelter, where he made a fire. He cooked some moose meat he had brought for his first night over the fire on a stick. For the remainder of the trip he would rely on a diet of pemmican. He crawled inside a comfortable sleeping bag made of caribou hide. Caribou hair is hollow and provides excellent insulation from the cold. He then placed a thick blanket of musk ox hide over him. This type of blanket would conserve more heat than any other animal hide because musk oxen live on the arctic tundra, the coldest of climates, year-round and have a pelt of thick guard hairs with an under layer of warm wool. He felt fortunate to have bartered with an Inuit man, exchanging several beaver and otter pelts for the blanket. He was now warm and comfortable in his small shelter. Isha took out his pipe and packed it with a thumb's length of tobacco. As he puffed the smoke, he watched the fire slowly dwindle to glowing coals. He felt that the day had gone well. His initial fear of the region had been dispelled.

It would be difficult and dangerous to travel where he was planning to go without the transport of a reliable dog team. He realized that he would be dependent on the dogs for his well-being from now on. He was pleased that he had spent so much time with the dogs in preparation for this journey. He puffed the remainder of his tobacco as he comfortably lay against the wall of the shelter. He had a sense of ease and optimism as he watched the small cloud of smoke lifting toward the top of the tepee before he drifted into sleep.

The next day Isha was up at dawn and had a breakfast of pemmican. Pemmican is made of dried moose meat pounded fine and mixed with melted tallow and berries. It is a dense, high-protein, high-energy food, and large amounts of it can be stored in a small area for many months and in some cases years. It can also be used as dog food. Twelve ounces provides around 3,500 calories. Isha would need two to three pemmican bars per day because of his high energy expenditure. Cici had made a large load of it and packed it in a leather satchel.

Isha removed the canvas from the shelter, fed the dogs, hooked them into their harnesses, and set off again. They stopped periodically to place traps off the shoreline of the lake. He saw several raised beaver lodges close to a frozen swamp. He chopped holes in the ice next to the lodges, placed a liquid scent to attract the beaver, and set the traps. He placed other traps next to otter burrows in the bank of the lake.

As they traveled over the frozen lake, Isha spied several caribou on the opposite shoreline. *How lucky*, he thought. He stopped the dogs and told them to lie down and stay. He put on a white canvas overcoat made for camouflage against the white backdrop of the frozen, snow-covered lake. He grabbed his rifle and then slowly crawled on his hands and knees through the snow to get within shooting range of the caribou. When he was close enough, he removed his fur mittens and took aim from a kneeling position. His hands were freezing as his fingers touched the cold steel of the rifle. He put any discomfort out of his mind and focused on the more important present task. He pointed his rifle at the largest of the caribou, aiming for the heart. The large animal was facing his direction but didn't appear alarmed. Isha needed the caribou to turn his side toward him for an adequate shot to the heart.

While he waited for the beast to turn, he quickly recognized the place and the situation. Flashing into his mind was a feeling that he had been here before, a recognition of the place in his deep subconscious. Yes! This situation was eerily like the dream of more than a year ago—the terrible dream in which he was killed by wolves. He remembered the situation in the middle of an unfamiliar frozen lake with a steep embankment on the other side, where he shot a caribou and was then set upon by a pack of wolves. He quickly looked around and saw nothing but the frozen expanse of the lake and the pine and spruce forests to the sides. Most importantly, he saw no wolves or any kind of movement. He put the fleeting thought out of his mind, thinking it silly. He then switched his thoughts to the business at hand as quickly as his feeling of déjà vu had entered his mind. He concentrated on sighting the rifle on the caribou.

He waited.

He waited.

He waited.

Steam rose from his exhalations in the cold air, which clouded his vision, so he held his breath. The caribou turned and exposed its side to Isha. Within a fraction of a second, Isha fired. He didn't register the rifle's recoil, only the moment of impact. The caribou staggered as if a great weight had come crashing down on it and then dropped immediately. It was a perfect shot, made with one bullet. Isha looked around again, thinking of his dream of a year ago, and still saw no sign of wolves.

Isha put on his mittens and ran back to the dog sled, where the dogs were still dutifully lying down in the same spot. He patted the dogs and said, "We're going to eat well tonight, boys!" Isha then drove the sled to the downed caribou. He again remembered his dream, in which he left the dog sled and walked a long distance toward the kill with dire consequences. The caribou was a bull with a large set of impressive antlers, again reminiscent of his dream. He looked around again, fearing what he might see, but again there was nothing but the lifeless vast frozen lake and silence except for the lonely sound of the wind whistling down the open expanse of the lake, stirring up small puffs of snow like dust on a desert. He stood silently for some time, cautiously scanning the horizon, before he proceeded to skin and butcher the animal, placing large quarters of meat in the sled.

Isha was an experienced hunter; it took him less than an hour to complete the job. He and his team then set off to complete the trapline. That evening Isha built another shelter, cooked a dinner of caribou heart, his favorite piece of meat, and fed the dogs portions of soft organ meat.

Things were working well. The dogs were doing a good job, he was placing traps in new areas where no one had been before, and the weather was cold and clear with no storms. Isha couldn't have asked for any better fortune so far.

After several days he finally reached the end point, over one hundred miles from where he had started. He again built a shelter for the night. In the future he planned to build a substantial cabin here at the end of his trapline for adequate resupply and rest. Isha gave his dogs an extra portion of caribou for a job well done. He ate a larger portion of roasted caribou than usual to reward himself for completing half the journey. The trip had been easy so far since he hadn't had to run the sled through bush trails. It was easy to follow a flat, open space along a frozen lakeshore, unencumbered by obstacles. He had seen no sign of wolves, and he wondered why he had ever doubted whether he should make the trip. He sat down on a stump by the dogs while they had dinner together and held a one-sided conversation with the dogs as if they could understand. The dogs looked at him quizzically with their ears erect as if they were interested in what he was saying. They seemed as happy as their master.

The next day Isha would begin the return trip to check on the many traps he had placed while working his way back to the village. He was anxious to see what he would find in the traps. He was hoping for mink, ermine, marten, fisher, fox, beaver, otter, and possibly lynx.

On his way back the next day, not far from where he had camped, he noticed a frozen waterfall coming from a precipitous hill on the other side of the lake. It was such a beautiful sight that he made a slight detour and drove over to it. He stopped close to the waterfall and looked to the top. He noted something dark on top of the hill close to the falls that triggered his curiosity. He wondered, *Could this be a cabin?* On closer inspection, it was clear that it was not a man-made structure. This dark object was so different from the surrounding topography in shape and color that he decided to investigate. He told the dogs to lie down and stay as he began climbing the steep hill.

When he finally reached the top, he saw that the dark object in front of him was a huge black rock with a flat surface, like a stage. The stone was dramatically different from the gray granite of the area and seemed curiously out of place, as if this huge black rock had come from the heavens and been purposefully placed here. He then realized what it was—the petrified giant black bear that had killed the Wendigo that Tiskigapon had told him about. He was taken aback when he looked at the evidence of the legend that most villagers thought was a fairy tale. He climbed the rock and viewed the vast expanse of the frozen lake directly adjacent to the frozen waterfall. He realized that he was standing on the sacred ground of his ancestors. He saw the dogs and the sled far below, appearing as tiny insects dutifully awaiting his return. He then raised his arms and looked up to the sky.

"Thank you, Great Spirit, for directing me here and showing me the way." He felt a rush of exhilaration. This rock was said to impart the strength and power of the giant bear to whoever stood upon it. Raising his arms to the heavens, he looked again over the vast lake and yelled at the top of his voice, hoping his ancestors would somehow hear him and be pleased, "This is my land now! The land of the Cree and the Clan of the Great Bear."

Isha decided to camp for the night below, next to the waterfall. He had enough food to get home to Lake Kashapon, and another day wouldn't make a difference in recovering his traps. He felt a strong urge to stay and investigate the area further. He built a small shelter, made a fire, ate some pemmican, fed the dogs, and had a comfortable night.

The next morning just before dawn, while the world was changing from black to gray, he climbed the precipitous rocky hill again and mounted the black rock. There he sat facing east, watching the sun slowly burn away the early-morning mist from the Seal River country like a doomed ghost. The sun rose slowly, as if it were too shy to meet the sky. He felt an aura of profound well-being. For once in his life, he felt that the Great Spirit was near him. His mind experienced a sharp clarity that he sensed only rarely, since his life was usually filled with mundane physical labor.

It was then that he saw a subtle thin, transparent veil between the rock and the surrounding country that seemed to shimmer slightly in the early-morning light. This was not a mist or a cloud but something he had never seen before. He rubbed his eyes, then closed and opened them again. The unusual phenomenon remained, covering everywhere he gazed. He remembered what Tiskigapon had said about the black rock being in a positive place of power and the remainder of the region in a negative one. Isha thought what he saw might be the boundary between the opposite forces of positive and negative energies. As the day wore on and the sun became brighter in the sky, the translucent, shimmering veil seemed to slowly dissipate from view.

The immediate area around the rock was so beautiful and had such a calming effect on him that he thought he would someday like to be buried in this place, facing east so that his spirit would sense the rising of the sun next to the top of the waterfall. He thought, *This is the ultimate place of peace.*

The Wolf

The frozen remains of the caribou carcass didn't go unnoticed. A large wolf pack that inhabited the area drew near shortly after the animal was brought down. Wolves' sense of smell is acute; they can smell even the smallest amount of blood from miles away. Although by human standards there was not much left of the slain animal, it was a fairly good meal for the wolves, who had no difficulty crushing the backbone for the bone marrow and the skull for the brain. The crushed bone itself is a good source of minerals and calcium for wolves. The discarded lower legs below the knee were also a nice treat.

Wolves have a tremendous bite strength at 1,500 pounds per square inch, with jaws specifically evolved to crush bone. They can crush a large moose femur in just two bites. The bite strength of a North American timber wolf is twice that of a large German shepherd dog and five times that of a human. Large wolves even have greater bite strength than that of African lions. Hyenas are the only land animal on earth with a bite stronger than that of North American timber wolves, but not by much. The brain size of a North American timber wolf is much larger than that of the average large dog, and wolves are thought to be much more intelligent than their canine cousins.

This was no ordinary northern timber wolf pack. Most packs average seven to ten wolves, but this was a "superpack" of around forty-five individuals. There were two main reasons for the large size of the pack. The first was the abundant amount of game in the area, which was on a major migration route of one of the largest caribou herds in Canada. The region had large wetland areas with shallow lakes, making it the perfect habitat for a large population of moose. Also, open areas of grassland were inhabited by wood bison and the occasional musk ox wandering south from the arctic tundra. Large as well as small game abounded.

However, probably the most important factor in the pack's success was the strong leadership of the alpha wolf, Mohegan. Wolves, like humans, hunt in a coordinated fashion, splitting up the pack to perform an ambush or driving game into an area from which the prey cannot retreat. This requires planning and knowledge of the prey, the capabilities of the pack, and the topography of the land. Wolves are ferocious predators who demonstrate masterful skill during a hunt. Their ability to bring down much larger and potentially more dangerous animals than themselves requires a coordinated teamwork approach orchestrated by the alpha wolf, or leader of the pack.

How an alpha wolf can communicate different hunting and killing strategies remains an enigma to science to this day. Wolves clearly have some type of communication that human beings are unaware of but that nonetheless is highly effective. Each member of the pack performs his or her own role during the hunt. This cooperation among the pack ensures success when hunting large prey. The male and female alpha pair set the rules for the hunt and care of the family. These rules are strictly followed by the rest of the pack, who behave like a well-trained military force. If the rules are broken or not well followed, there could be dire consequences for the disobedient wolf.

In most packs, the alpha pair mate for life, and the alpha female is usually the only one to bear pups, usually once per year. The alpha male and female are excellent parents. The pups, like human children, are routinely brought toys, such as sticks, pieces of bone, fur, or pieces of antler, for them to play with and investigate. The yearling wolves act as babysitters while the rest of the pack is on the hunt. The entire pack, however, is intimately involved in the care and instruction of the pups. Wolf society is a classic example of communal care. Roughly half of Mohegan's superpack were family members. The others were an assortment of original members of the pack, members of smaller packs who had lost their alpha wolf and then been absorbed, or lone wolves who had been driven from their initial pack. All, however, were totally dedicated to Mohegan as their leader. In wolf society, full bellies create a loyal following.

Rarely an animal is born with physical and mental abilities far above those of the usual animal of its kind, just as some people are born with more intelligence and some with much greater physical strength than others. Mohegan was one of these rare unique and gifted animals. He was either a mutation or a large jump in the evolution of the species. He was much larger than the usual male North American timber wolf, weighing a bit more than 240 pounds. He had a large chest and torso that had the ability to conserve heat even in the coldest temperatures and the ability to knock down large prey with just a blow from his body. Mohegan's head was nearly twice the size of that of an average wolf, with large jaws and teeth creating twice the biting capacity. He was able to cause deep, gaping wounds with a single bite. The size of his bite was more comparable to that of a large bear than that that of a wolf. His long, thin legs were perfectly made to run at high speeds even in deep snow. The paws of timber wolves are large, perfectly adapted for running on snow, like snowshoes for humans. Mohegan was faster than most, able to run at speeds up to forty miles per hour for prolonged periods. The endurance of timber wolves is renowned. They can bring down prey after running for many hours, and at times days, essentially wearing the prey animals down through the pack's extraordinary endurance and persistence.

This wolf pack had no difficulty in bringing down the largest of animals. Each wolf is somehow instructed by the alpha to lunge at the prey, inflict a rapid bite, and then retreat quickly while other wolves do the same from many different directions. The key is to cause a quick, deep injury but to avoid being gored, kicked, or damaged by a large musk ox, caribou, bison, or moose. Slowly the prey animal wears down from fatigue and blood loss, at which time the entire pack quickly closes in on the defenseless, exhausted animal. One of the wolves, usually Mohegan, would then lunge for the neck and quickly finish the animal by crushing its neck and trachea, causing quick suffocation. Depending on the situation, however, Mohegan was sometimes known to bring down a large prey animal himself without help from the pack because of his extraordinary strength and speed. Mohegan was no ordinary wolf.

In addition to his great physical abilities Mohegan was intelligent. He had the unique ability to know when a chase would or would not be successful. If the prey was too strong to run down, he would quickly terminate the hunt and conserve the pack's energy for a more successful hunt later. In nature, energy conservation and expenditure are life-and-death concepts. Mohegan was acutely aware of this.

Before Mohegan became the alpha wolf, things had not been as good for the pack. There were only nine wolves, and most of the time they were on the verge of starvation even though the region had a plentiful supply of game. The pack frequently ended up in futile chases, wearing the wolves down. During a hunt there were frequently stragglers spread out on the trail because of weakness and unhealed wounds, diminishing the pack's effectiveness. There was bickering and internal dissension, creating poor morale and less effective hunting. These problems were due to a weak alpha leader named Nagan.

The pack was in dire straits. There was only one surviving pup, a female named Sinapu, out of three litters. Sinapu's siblings had been killed in an attack by a large bear who discovered the den. The pack was too weak from malnutrition to defend their own pups. The next two litters died because the alpha female couldn't produce enough milk to sustain them. It was a time of misery for the pack.

Through eons of time, natural selection had created genetically programmed behavioral traits focused on making a successful pack, which meant sharing food equally. Wolves don't usually bicker or fight over food like their distant cousins, dogs. Not sharing food from a kill would not only diminish the pack's strength because of a lack of nutrition but also cause disunity among its members, decreasing cooperation during a hunt.

Nagan had a special dislike of Mohegan, even though he was barely three years old and not an obvious threat. Despite Mohegan's youth, he was as large as an adult wolf. He was rangy and sinewy but lacked the bulk and muscle that were to come. Nagan refused to allow Mohegan to feed at any kill, even though Mohegan had participated in the hunt and takedown of the prey. As soon as Mohegan began feeding, Nagan would lunge at him, forcing him away. Instead of showing submission by yelping, putting his tail between his legs, and running away, Mohegan would turn and face Nagan without emotion. There was no snarling, bristling, or showing of the fangs. He simply walked away from the kill. He refused to grovel at Nagan's feet and become subservient to a tyrant whom he despised. He was determined to bide his time and not provoke an all-out fight at his early age. Mohegan's nonreaction angered Nagan even further. He didn't want to start an overt fight with the young wolf for fear of injury, even though he knew he would likely be victorious.

There was something noble in Mohegan's nature that refused to be suppressed. The flickering flame of greatness could not be extinguished, although it had yet to be fully realized. It was probably Mohegan's strength of character that Nagan felt was a future threat to his leadership. Even though Mohegan was seething inside for revenge, he knew he couldn't risk attacking a mature wolf when he was not fully grown. In a fight Mohegan probably had the physical ability to depose Nagan. However, he lacked the confidence and mental and emotional ability to do so. Mohegan never knew a moment of security or comfort at this time. His life was continuous hunger and harassment. Nagan's goal was to slowly kill Mohegan or drive him away.

Mohegan's life hadn't always been this way. He remembered long ago being loved and cared for by his mother and father, making him an emotionally strong young pup. But that was long ago, and now they were gone. He had no one to protect him from the malignancy of Nagan.

Wolves are highly social animals and need others of their kind to be content and thrive. The best friends Mohegan had were Wachak, another young wolf of the same age who had played with Mohegan since they were puppies, and Sinapu, a yearling female wolf, younger than the other two. Sinapu was precocious and skilled despite her age and participated in the hunt. While growing up, the three bonded closely. They slept close together and hunted as a team, developing excellent communication skills and frequently ignoring Nagan's directives. The three were more efficient in bringing down prey than Nagan and the older wolves despite their youth and meager nutrition. But they lacked the strength of fully mature wolves as well as numbers, which led to lengthy and energy-expending chases. If not for these three, however, the pack would have starved.

Any wolf showing interest in Mohegan was viciously attacked by the tyrannical alpha wolf, thus depriving Mohegan of any social interaction in a continued slow, persistent effort to drive him away. Wachak and Sinapu resented the persecution of Mohegan, but there was nothing they could do against the more powerful Nagan.

Mohegan would steal some bone, skin, or a small piece of meat from a recent kill before being attacked by Nagan, but it was not nearly enough. He was slowly starving, becoming weaker every day. Mohegan was an outcast within his own pack. He became morose and solitary, silently brooding as the others fed on a kill in which he was not allowed to participate.

Mohegan realized that he needed to do something to save himself. One day when the pack were feeding at a kill with Mohegan on the periphery, Mohegan noticed mice running into a small burrow. He crawled stealthily close to the burrow and with great patience waited in ambush for a mouse to emerge. With lightning-like speed, he grabbed the first mouse that came out. He repeated this maneuver and made a meal out of multiple mice. It wasn't a huge meal, but it was enough to stave off starvation for a while.

Having been totally absorbed by hunting large game, he had never before realized how abundant mice and other small animals were in his environment. He adapted the hunting techniques he learned from ambushing mice to rabbits, ground squirrels, lemmings, and many other smaller animals that wolves don't usually hunt. He became skilled in the ways and habits of small animals and became an effective predator. He hunted alone and in secret, finding certain open grassy areas that were more populated with rodents and became adept at digging out their burrows. He supplemented his diet with an occasional larger meal, such as a weasel or even a fox.

He killed a large male wolverine that gave him a substantial meal for several days, but at great cost from a hard-fought battle with the nimble predator whose claws and fangs left him wounded. Wolverines, pound for pound, are the most vicious and fearsome animal in the north woods. Normally wolves or even bears would not attempt to attack a wolverine; however, at this point Mohegan didn't care if he lived or died. He was looking for a fight. It did give him good experience in combat with an agile and dangerous foe. The fight left him exhausted. He concluded that fighting another predator, especially a wolverine, as a lone wolf was not worth the energy expended unless it was necessary.

Mohegan stayed away from the pack, making only occasional forays into their midst. These infrequent visits stopped after a few months. Nagan couldn't understand why Mohegan appeared so healthy and not emaciated like the rest of the pack.

Mohegan became a successful solitary lone wolf for several years. He usually slept at the top of a large, rocky hill barren of trees so that he could detect any potential prey in the vicinity. He occasionally glimpsed his old pack in the distance on a hunt and longed to be with them. Like a human prisoner in solitary confinement, he ached to be with his family and friends.

One night, in a fit of profound sadness, he raised his head toward a bright full moon and gave a long, lonely howl that resounded throughout the region as if echoing through a long canyon. He continued to howl for nearly half an hour. This was Mohegan's way of crying. The dejected sound was heard by Wachak and Sinapu, who both raised their heads from their curled, sleeping bodies as their ears became erect. The sound pierced them with despair, the depths of which could be felt only in the middle of night. The two wolves looked at each other, and both wanted to go to Mohegan, but their instinct to stay with the pack overwhelmed their deep personal desire to be with their friend. Nagan also heard the howling and was pleased that he had driven this potential competitor away. The howl was not only heard by animals; the sound carried as far as the distant Lake Kashapon, where it was faintly heard by Isha looking out on the lake, giving him a shiver up his spine and a feeling of deep dread.

After howling at the moon, Mohegan lay down and from that moment on was determined to have a change of heart. He was done with grieving. Never again would he howl in sadness. He detached himself from the world with a steely focus. He would no longer concern himself with grief, pity, or any kind of weakness. These emotions disgusted him. He would no longer think of family or friends, as these thoughts could leave him vulnerable to emotional pain. That night, he hardened his heart and became machinelike, content with his solitary world but planning to one day seek revenge.

One day when Mohegan was stalking a rabbit lying low in the grass, a female caribou ambled close to him, oblivious to his presence. Mohegan saw his chance and gave chase by instinct. He closed on the caribou with a burst of speed and lunged for the neck. With his mighty jaws he pulled the animal down with a powerful jerk of his muscular neck and shoulders. Mohegan was amazed at himself. He had not only outrun the caribou but single-handedly pulled her down. This boosted his confidence immensely. He began to chase entire herds of caribou, selecting the weakest of the group to take down. Many times he would drive groups of caribou into box canyons, where he knew they would be trapped until he selected his victim.

After bringing down many other big game animals by himself with relative ease, he was entirely self-sufficient. He had achieved hunting expertise for all animals great and small.

As time passed, he became larger, quicker, craftier, and deadlier. He was no longer the skinny adolescent. His body had a bulk of thick, hard muscle. He was now a force to be reckoned with, and he knew it. However, he needed the socialization of the pack to be truly fulfilled, and he felt an instinctive need to carry on his bloodline. He was an entirely different creature, physically, mentally, and emotionally, from the one who had been driven away. It was now his time.

Wachak, Sinapu, and the rest of the pack saw a large animal

slowly walking toward them through the trees. Initially it appeared as a large, dark, indistinct shadow. They rose to their feet and watched with interest as it drew near. At first they didn't know what it was because it was so large. Their initial impression was that a bear was coming at them, which caused some alarm. They had experienced a bear attack some years ago that had resulted in the killing of several pups from the den, but there were no pups now to be concerned about. Silent ripples of anxiety spread through the pack as they gazed at the dark creature slowly coming their way. As it gradually drew closer, they suddenly recognized Mohegan.

He had changed dramatically. Mohegan was now nearly twice his previous size. He was so large that he appeared to be not a wolf but something far more fearsome. Several of the wolves wanted to greet him after his long absence with wagging tails and licks to the face but didn't dare for fear of Nagan's retribution. Mohegan ignored the other wolves, calmly walking past them as if they didn't exist. His gaze was intently focused straight ahead on the alpha wolf. He was outwardly calm, but his inner soul was wound tight as a metal spring, ready to unleash a powerful malignant force. He stalked over to Nagan, who was sniffing the ground for a scent. Nagan raised his head and looked at a huge wolf he didn't immediately recognize. The sudden appearance of a strange wolf before him sent a rush of surprise and aggression through him.

Before Nagan could react, without warning and within an instant, Mohegan lunged at his neck and jerked the tissue away, slashing it open. Nagan's body was flung into the air like a limp rag doll by Mohegan's enormous strength. The huge bite left a gaping hole, as if it had been slashed by an exquisitely sharp samurai knife. Nagan was down on the ground within seconds, bleeding to death and gasping for air because of the gash in his windpipe. The pack was astounded at the ferocity of the attack. It was a lightening flash of slaughter.

Mohegan stood over the downed Nagan and looked at the other pack members, effectively saying, *I'm in charge now! Follow my orders or you'll get the same treatment.* Cold revenge had finally been served. Mohegan had killed Nagan with ease and with deadly efficiency. There had been no buildup of emotion or squabbling between the two prior to the assassination, as in most challenges for power. It had not even been a fight, as Nagan had had no idea what was coming. As far as he knew, Mohegan was not an issue. In his mind, the younger wolf had been driven from the pack and was now a subservient wolf who occasionally visited despite being continuously harassed.

The rest of the wolf pack were stunned. They had seen dominance battles before, but nothing like this. Struggles for the dominant alpha position usually resulted in a brutal fight, many times lasting hours, with the victor frequently being damaged as well as the loser. The loser was usually not killed but simply demoted to a subservient position or at most banished from the pack.

The pack gathered in a large circle and looked at the dead wolf. They had witnessed what they would have thought was impossible. Wachak, Mohegan's lifelong friend, was the first to come over to Mohegan and brush against his body as a sign of fealty to the new leader. The remainder of the pack came to Mohegan with their heads down and tails wagging as signs of submission. Several wolves even began licking Mohegan's face. All allegiance to Nagan instantly vanished. The dead former alpha wolf then became a meal for the hungry pack. Mohegan could have injured Nagan or just chased him away, but he wanted to make a clear example of him for the rest of the pack to heed and remember.

Mohegan ruled the pack with an iron fist. Under Mohegan's leadership, the pack grew rapidly and became stronger and healthier. It became an efficient and well-managed killing machine. He treated his pack members well if they showed subservience to him. If they didn't, it could mean their life within an instant, and all knew it.

As in any military organization, the general was only as good as his second-in-command. Wachak proved to be excellent in this regard. They considered each other brothers. Wachak was not nearly as large or strong as Mohegan, but he had leadership capability. He respected Mohegan's abilities and communicated exceptionally well with the big alpha wolf. During a hunt, Wachak knew Mohegan's plan of action and was able to implement these hunting strategies to perfection. Wachak knew when to split off, taking half of the pack away to surround the prey in an ambush while Mohegan and the rest of the pack gave chase, driving the prey toward Wachak's waiting group.

Occasionally Mohegan would sprint just beyond a prey animal because of his exceptional speed, then turn abruptly, jump, and grab the neck of the doomed animal to bring it down unassisted with one powerful movement. This was an example of the strength and speed that none of the pack members could duplicate. What was even more amazing to the pack was that the prey animal taken down by Mohegan could be healthy and strong—it didn't necessarily have to be in a weakened condition. Mohegan was able to kill other animals as easily as humans kill mosquitos.

To feed such a large pack, they needed to make a kill at least every two to three days. For this pack with its outstanding leader, this was not a problem. After the pack made a kill, an individual wolf could ingest as much as twenty pounds of meat in a single sitting. After such a feast, the pack would rest.

There was one animal that Mohegan feared and respected above all others—man! He'd had a traumatic experience when he was just a yearling wolf. His father, who was the alpha wolf at the time, had been shot and killed by a man. This had resulted in his mother being driven away from the pack by the new alpha male, Nagan, and his new alpha female. Wolves without a pack usually do not fare well in the harsh conditions of the subarctic. Mohegan was an exception.

Mohegan had witnessed the killing of his father by the man. He remembered the man raising a stick to his shoulder from far away and hearing the loud thunder-like noise, followed by a hole made in his father's side, killing him instantly. Mohegan didn't understand how a man could be so far away and yet kill without touching his victim. He concluded that the man's special stick was magic. He subsequently tried to avoid any contact with humans because of their dangerous and mysterious abilities. Unlike others of his kind, Mohegan knew man was an animal, not some mystical being with superpowers. Mohegan thought a man alone was weak and easily killed if not for his magic stick, which he did not understand except for its deadly consequences. He thought the magic stick shot an invisible horn that could put a hole in any animal from a great distance. It was much more deadly than being gored by a musk ox or bull moose at close range.

He understood that man is a pack leader to lesser animals such as dogs and uses them as his slaves. These lowly slave dogs made life easier and safer because of man's basic physical weakness. Man needed to wear the skins of other animals to survive in the cold. Mohegan therefore thought man was not meant to live in this environment and thus was an invader that shouldn't be in this country.

Mohegan had a poor opinion of dogs. He recognized their kinship to wolves but considered them weak and stupid. They were noisy and made sounds from emotion when there was no need for communication. They mindlessly barked for no reason at objects such as moving leaves or other inconsequential things. He noted that dogs came in various sizes and shapes, but nonetheless all were dogs and all inferior. He considered dogs instruments used by man and therefore an enemy that should be killed.

The Invasion

While the pack was on the hunt following a herd of caribou, Mohegan heard a faint, far-distant sound. He immediately stopped the chase, turned his head in the direction of the sound with his ears erect, and listened intently. He was frozen like a statue in his alertness. All was silent except for the cold north wind blowing through the trees. The other pack members looked quizzically at Mohegan. They obviously didn't hear the subtle, far-off sound. Mohegan stood still in silent, rigid attention, nose in the air. The other wolves looked at one another anxiously. They were confused and somewhat disappointed since they were on the verge of taking down a large, wounded caribou. They hadn't fed in four days and were hungry. They didn't understand why Mohegan had abruptly stopped the hunt and was acting so strangely.

Then they heard the barely audible, far-off sound of a wolf howling, followed by a second howl, faint but clear. With the last distant sound of a wolf, an immediate sense of alarm and anger coursed through Mohegan's body. His fur bristled, and he gave a low growl as he looked at the pack behind him. The wolf pack finally heard the distant sound and turned their heads toward Mohegan. With Mohegan's momentary glance at them, they knew what was to be done. Mohegan turned away from the caribou hunt and began trotting in the direction of the sound. The entire hunting group turned and followed their leader without question. They immediately lost all thought of the caribou and their hunger. They knew what their duty was, and they were ready.

Wolves are fiercely territorial. Mohegan was now completely focused on a new objective—to find the other pack of wolves and eliminate them. Over several hours, Mohegan, with robotic coolness, steadily came closer to the distant howls. There are many types of howls and barks that wolves give describing their emotion or communicating. The howls emanating from the other pack were of gleeful happiness and victory over a new kill. Because of the type of sound Mohegan heard, he knew he would have the element of surprise.

The pack, with Mohegan in the lead, was loping along crowded together in one large group, touching and brushing against one another as they moved in close formation. This instinctual grouping helped them gain confidence and solidarity for an anticipated fight. This was not their usual spread-out hunting formation. The pack had never experienced a confrontation with another pack before. It would be nothing like attacking a herd of caribou or even a large moose. They all knew this was going to be different and potentially dangerous. Their instinct was guiding them to war. They had no hesitation, no thinking, no questioning of other options. It was what nature demanded of them, like birds migrating south for the winter or caribou migrating north for the summer. The pack was following their trusted alpha leader as loyal soldiers. It was to be a savage, dangerous battle for dominance, a gang fight of the worst kind. They knew they were going up against the same type of savage viciousness and killing fangs that they themselves possessed. It was a prelude to a war with no mercy. They were willing to give their lives for their trusted alpha leader and their pack. As they loped in the direction of the sound of the other pack, each member felt a building communal spirit of silent ferocity and mindless hate. They were now fully confident and focused to finish off their deadly adversaries in the most brutal way possible.

After over an hour Mohegan stopped and sniffed their surroundings. These new wolves had the audacity to mark this area as their own territory with their scent. He could tell by the scent that it was not just one or two individuals foraging alone but a pack of both males and females. Mohegan's blood began to boil. This other pack knew exactly what they were doing. This was no accident of a few wolves inadvertently wandering into his territory. This was a serious invasion, an attempted takeover of his realm.

Other wolf packs are competitors for food as well as potential killers of pack's pups if their den is discovered. Other canines such as coyotes, foxes, or dogs would all be considered deadly enemies, warranting immediate attack, by the resident wolf pack. There was no prospect of anything but complete annihilation if Mohegan had his way.

Mohegan and the pack were getting closer. He could hear wolves ahead in a small valley, feeding on a recent kill. Mohegan and one group went one way, and Wachak with another group went the opposite way, making a complete circle around the unsuspecting feeding interlopers. All escape routes were shut off, guarded by members of Mohegan's pack. Mohegan stood on a small hill, looking down into the valley around seventy yards away. His wolf pack were excited and couldn't wait to pounce on their unsuspecting enemy. They knew there would be a bloodbath since they greatly outnumbered their opponents and had Mohegan, the giant and deadly alpha leader, on their side.

Anxiety to start the attack was slowly building. They stood on the crest of the hill, nervously fidgeting with anticipation. Their gazes were fixed on the unsuspecting enemy—twelve wolves in the valley feeding on a recently killed moose. However, they were disciplined and awaited Mohegan's order. The invading wolves were oblivious to the impending threat to their lives. The smaller pack had often confronted other wolf packs and had always been successful in driving them away and usurping other packs' territories. They had always been victorious because they were more aggressive and audacious than other packs. This group knew a fight was coming; they just didn't know when, and they weren't expecting the fight so soon while enjoying their feast. They were fully confident that when the fight came, they would be successful, as in all the others they had experienced in the past.

The alpha of the group was named Talgu. He was above average in size and extremely aggressive and had never been beaten. His ferocity and confidence were unparalleled. He thought he was entering the territory of Nagan's old pack, which he knew was much weaker than his. Little did he know that things had changed dramatically from when Nagan had led his pack in this area. He felt confident that the new territory would be easy to take. He had planned to expand his territory and the size of his pack into this region of bounty with an abundance of game. Talgu had no idea what was lying in wait on the surrounding hills.

Talgu's pack several years before had come across a starved refugee lone she-wolf who had been driven out by Nagan. Talgu's pack was successful and well fed, and its numbers were slowly growing. The refugee wolf could tell that this pack was healthy and could accommodate her. She wanted to join the new pack for her own safety and survival. She knew that approaching a strange new pack was risky, but she had no choice since she could not survive on her own in the harsh subarctic environment. This wolf was Mohegan's mother. She came to Talgu in a submissive posture, her head down and tail between her legs, giving a slight whimper. The pack surrounded the pitiful wolf, staring at her in silence. The she-wolf tried to slowly lick Talgu's lower lip as she cowered before him. Talgu looked at the pitiful refugee and without warning lunged at her. The rest of the pack followed his lead and attacked Mohegan's starving mother, who was quickly dispatched and left on the ground for the scavengers. It would have been easy to chase the starved wolf away, which is what usually happens. However, Talgu was particularly vicious and enjoyed killing, even when there was no need. He knew this would be an easy kill and wished to show his power to the rest of the pack.

Mohegan had never fought another wolf except Nagan, which had not really been a fight but rather a quick assassination. He was confident of winning but was concerned about possible injury, which could impair his ability to lead the pack. Fighting a wolf was not like taking down any other animal, like a moose or a caribou. From the hill overlooking the valley where Talgu's pack was feeding, he correctly identified the alpha leader. Mohegan thought this new alpha wolf was a potentially dangerous adversary. To minimize any casualties to his pack, his plan was to quickly kill Talgu; then the rest of Talgu's pack would lose heart and flee, only to be destroyed. On the other hand, Mohegan realized that if he were killed, no matter what the odds were, his pack would likely be defeated and dissolve into smaller separate groups, destroying the superpack structure. The question was how to quickly dispatch a dangerous alpha wolf without injury to himself. Mohegan knew he was dealing with an aggressive and confident alpha male since the other wolf had so flagrantly crossed into his territory without a care. Because of Talgu's aggressive behavior, Mohegan concluded that Talgu would attack him quickly. Mohegan planned to let Talgu make the first move, exposing himself for a devastating counterattack.

Suddenly Talgu caught the scent of Mohegan and the surrounding pack of over forty wolves. His head abruptly rose out of the carcass, nose in the air and ears erect. A generalized alarm among the other twelve wolves became apparent. They all raised their heads. The fur on all their backs bristled. They bared their teeth and emitted a communal low growl. They had not seen Mohegan's pack yet, but they knew other wolves were close. They had no idea of the numbers against them lurking on the adjacent hills just out of sight. They were not overly fearful of the newly detected other pack. They were ready and willing to follow Talgu into battle at any time, as they had many times before. The expected confrontation was coming sooner than they had anticipated, but that didn't matter because they were ready.

Before they could react, Mohegan gave a bark and all forty-five wolves charged down the hill at full speed. The smaller pack had a sudden spasm of dread and fear as they saw the number of wolves pouring down the hillside, like an avalanche of bristling fur and teeth in all directions. They had never seen anything like this before. Panic spread like a bolt of lightning through Talgu's pack. Mohegan's pack jumped on the unsuspecting wolves within seconds before they could mount any defense or retreat. A ferocious, slashing melee of blood, fangs, and fur ensued. The air was filled with the horrible, unworldly loud yelps, growls, and screams of over fifty wolves in a life-and-death struggle. The frightful sound was as if hell itself had opened and armies of demonic spirits had emerged. These terrifying sounds of death, anger, and carnage could be heard for miles around. Other animals in the area lifted their heads and listened fearfully to the deadly event that was transpiring.

Mohegan quickly sought out the leader of the invading pack. Talgu was initially shocked at Mohegan's size, but that didn't deter him from thinking that he would kill the larger wolf. His thoughts were like Mohegan's: if he could kill Mohegan, it would demoralize his opponent's pack, who could then be defeated despite their greater numbers.

Just as Mohegan had predicted, Talgu was quick and aggressive. He lunged at Mohegan first, leaving his neck exposed. Mohegan, in an extraordinary feat of athleticism, parried the thrust of Talgu's open jaws by jumping into the air over his attacker's head. Mohegan opened his huge jaws and came down on the back of Talgu's neck. Mohegan's steel-trap-like teeth instantaneously penetrated the deep tissue. With one bite, Mohegan crushed Talgu's cervical vertebrae and spinal cord, leaving Talgu instantly paralyzed from the neck down but awake and fully aware. Talgu gave a bloodcurdling high-pitched screech, a pitiful sound he had never uttered before, which was heard throughout the area. Talgu's pack recognized their leader's scream and lost all heart for the fight. Talgu crumpled to the ground in a motionless heap. Mohegan deplored Talgu's arrogance and lack of judgment, which were unbecoming of an alpha leader. He correctly thought Talgu was overconfident to the point of dangerous arrogance, as he had needlessly placed his pack in harm's way.

The unfortunate wolf lay on the ground paralyzed, making small, muffled yelps for help. Mohegan placed his huge paw over the paralyzed wolf's head and pushed it into the ground as a humiliating act of dominance over his vanquished foe. Mohegan stood over Talgu, snarling and baring his fangs. He placed his sharp teeth mere inches from Talgu's face. Talgu could feel Mohegan's hot breath, which elicited a terror he had never known before. Furrows appeared on Mohegan's nose, and the hair on his back bristled. Mohegan thought that an alpha leader should be judged by a higher standard than others in the pack and therefore should be given no mercy. Mohegan despised poor alpha leadership. He had seen the effects on the rest of the pack from his experience with Nagan. He knew the pain and suffering that a poor alpha wolf could bring to the members of a pack.

Talgu was undeserving of a quick, honorable death. Mohegan turned and walked away. This was the signal for the rest of the pack to finish the job. They quickly jumped on the helpless Talgu and began crushing his bones and tearing out his visceral organs while

Talgu was still alive and aware. Talgu, because of his severed spinal cord, could do nothing but lie on the ground and feel his enemies devouring him. Over ten wolves were tearing at Talgu at once, jerking his body in multiple directions while Mohegan watched with malignant satisfaction.

Mohegan was a master of the kill, and this had been an easy one. Once Talgu's pack saw their leader destroyed with ease, they tried to flee in all directions, but to no avail. They were all chased down by gangs of their enemies, who severely mauled and then killed them without mercy. After the destruction was complete, the victorious wolves came to Mohegan, happy and wagging their tails. They brushed against him with their bodies, licking him in congratulations and adulation for the victorious leader. The entire pack huddled together and raised their heads to the sky, howling in unison and yelping to celebrate their victory. The haunting voices of over forty wolves reverberated throughout the hills and valleys for miles around, striking dread and fear in any animal that heard the bloodthirsty sound.

It had been an overwhelming victory, a slaughter of their unlucky rivals. A wise and cautious alpha wolf would have sent scouts or investigated the new territory himself before committing the entire pack to a kill in another's territory. The borders of the territory were routinely patrolled and clearly marked with Mohegan's scent. Nature is unforgiving and does not suffer fools with poor judgment.

The victorious pack had a meal of their rivals, ripping and tearing their flesh apart and crushing their bones. The victorious wolves' heads were covered in blood from the great feast. Usually wolves clean their faces of blood and scraps by rubbing themselves in the snow or grass, but not now. They seemed to relish the sight of their reddened faces as a sign of victory, almost as if they were soldiers wearing medals for bravery won in battle. The pack seemed to enjoy this meal above all the others. Their satisfaction in feasting on the carcasses of their vanquished foes was heightened because the meat they were ingesting was that of a hated enemy, killed in combat.

The Old Moose

After Mohegan's pack had spent nearly a week digesting the feast of their rival wolves and the moose the other pack had killed, it was time to go on the hunt again. Mohegan got up from lying around the den and issued several yips and barks to which the rest of the pack immediately responded, ending their week of leisure. They followed Mohegan in a direction they hadn't taken in some time. The country they were heading for was a low, swampy area heavily covered in willows, which moose love to eat. The pack immediately knew they were on the hunt for moose. They fanned out to cover a large area in search of their prey, with Wachak at one end of the pack and Mohegan at the other. They searched all day, covering large swaths of territory without success.

Dusk was approaching when Mohegan heard Wachak's bark/howl, which was then repeated by several other wolves. Mohegan and the rest of the wolves turned in the direction of their comrades' call and raced through the brush toward them. They covered nearly a mile in just a few minutes, anticipating a hunt of a prey animal in progress. When Mohegan and the rest caught up with Wachak's group, they were not disappointed. They were in hot pursuit of a large bull moose. Mohegan was able to catch up to the moose, running alongside him stride for stride. He was now able to better evaluate the physical condition of the moose. Usually a healthy bull moose can fight off an attacking wolf pack or cause so much potential damage to the wolves that it would not be worth their effort to bring it down. This moose was enormous, over eight feet tall at the shoulder, and weighed well over a thousand pounds. Its antlers could have held Mohegan like a cradle. It was probably the largest moose he had ever seen. However, the moose was old and weak. Its strength was starting to diminish as the wolves chased close behind. Its legs quivered with each large step in its irregular gallop. The pack knew the old moose wouldn't be able to sustain the chase for long.

The moose started to slow down despite his strenuous efforts to keep going. The wolves noticed heavy rapid breathing. There was a thick white froth around his mouth, and his tongue was sticking out, indicating the moose was beginning to tire. The fatigue of old age was now obvious. The moose then lost his footing and fell but quickly recovered. Wachak and the other wolves were biting his legs, delivering deep, slashing gashes. The big moose stood up and started running again, but now he was limping, and his gait was even more unsteady. He felt his strength slowly starting to ebb. He knew he had to take a different approach to defend himself. He tried to kick the wolves behind him with his enormous hind legs. A kick from a large moose, even an old one, could severely injure or even kill a wolf.

When the moose was younger, he could have kept running all day or turned and fought the wolves off, as he had done many times before. He mourned for those days, when he had taken pride in defending himself, fighting off countless wolf attacks. However, he knew those days were gone. The inevitable outcome was obvious, but he would keep fighting to the very end. His pride and dignity would not let him give up and lie down. If he was going down, he was going down fighting, with honor. He hoped he could injure or kill a wolf one last time before he died.

In the past the old moose had been the king of his domain, ruling over an extensive territory and fighting and driving away many other bull moose. He'd had a harem of cow moose and had sired countless calves, populating the entire region with his gene pool, but now was the end of his long reign.

Mohegan saw the courage of the old moose. He understood it and respected the old moose for a valiant fight. Mohegan knew the old moose didn't have much time left in his life, and he realized that the old moose knew this as well. Mohegan wanted to do the old moose a favor by delivering a quick death instead of a slow and painful one in some swampy bog, unable to move, being slowly eaten away by parasites and insects before the eventual demise he knew was coming in just a few months. Mohegan realized that one day something like this could happen to him. He would make the kill as quick and painless as possible.

The leg wounds now crippled the huge beast, severing the tendons so he could no longer run. The moose was so tall that his vulnerable neck was too high for the pack to easily attack. The moose turned, facing Wachak and the others with his oversized sharp antlers. He lunged at his tormentors with the last bit of strength that he could muster. Instead of jumping away to safety, Wachak stood his ground, knowing that the moose would need to lower his head and expose his vulnerable neck to Mohegan and the others for a final fatal attack. Wachak knew he would have to absorb a dangerous and potentially fatal blow by the moose for it to be taken down. The moose hit Wachak like a speeding truck hitting a stationary pedestrian on a street, sending his body hurtling through the air and hitting the ground hard yards away. Wachak fell on his side, stunned but not seriously injured. The old moose felt a fleeting sense of pride for the last time at throwing an attacking wolf so far and hopefully killing or injuring him. Mohegan saw his opportunity and flung himself at the old moose's lowered neck with great force and momentum. He had timed his jump perfectly. His jaws clamped down on the moose's neck and, with Mohegan's blow to the body, knocked the moose to its side with a loud, reverberating thud like that of a huge tree falling in the forest.

It is an extremely rare feat for a wolf to knock a large bull moose down with a body blow, but Mohegan was no ordinary wolf. The rest of the pack jumped on the old moose and finished him within minutes. It was an excellent kill, performed with perfection by skilled killers. With this much meat from such a large animal, the pack would probably not need to hunt for over a week. Mohegan walked over to the still dazed Wachak and licked his face as he brushed against his body. This was a sign of concern and gratitude for taking a heavy blow for the benefit of the pack. Wachak slowly got to his feet and shook his body. He ambled toward the downed moose with his friend Mohegan by his side.

The Bear

While the pack was feeding on the moose, Mohegan, always acutely aware of his surroundings, heard something move in the nearby bush. He heard tree branches breaking and leaves rustling as if a large boulder were slowly rolling through the forest. As he raised his head from the kill, he spied something large and dark making its way through the forest. A large male bear emerged out of the bush. The bear stopped for a moment as he and the giant wolf locked their gazes upon one another. There was an immediate recognition of two hated mortal enemies. Instinctive feelings of aggression arose in both top predators. Without hesitation, the bear bolted at full speed toward the downed moose and the wolves. His movements were fluid and swift despite his enormous bulk. His muscles rippled across his humped back, causing the fur to undulate in waves.

The bear jumped on top of the carcass, looming over it with an intimidating powerful presence, scattering the wolves like frightened birds. He opened his gaping jaws, baring his huge teeth, and delivered a fearful bellowing sound that reverberated throughout the area. This show of force intimidated the wolf pack, but not Mohegan. The wolves held at a safe distance from the bear, looking at one another and wondering what was to transpire.

Mohegan knew this bear well. His name was Otho, and he had been in the area for many years. Otho was vicious and frequently killed not for hunger but just for the thrill. He especially liked to kill bear cubs that were not of his lineage so the mother would later be receptive for him to mate with, thus continuing his own gene pool. He frequently stalked mother bears with cubs for days. He could usually handle the mother prior to killing and eating her cubs. This was his preferred source of meat if he could find and catch them.

However, if he could locate and follow a wolf pack, it would be easy for him to obtain a large, recently killed meat source with minimal effort. This bear had frequently terrorized and stalked Nagan's old pack when Mohegan was young. The routine for Nagan's pack was to make the kill and eat as quickly as possible before Otho showed up and chased them away. This usually caused the pack to eat only one-third or half of the carcass before the bear came upon them. It was one of the many reasons why Nagan's pack was always hungry and frequently on the verge of starvation. The bear had once raided the den of Nagan's pack and killed all but one of the wolf pups. Putting up with a short period of minor harassment by the wolves until he could brush them away from a kill was routine for Otho.

Mohegan now faced the dilemma of how to deal with this dangerous threat to his pack. Now that Otho knew the wolves were in the area, he would become a parasite on the pack and a terrible threat to the pack's pups if he discovered the den.

Mohegan had hated Otho ever since he was a youth. He had seen what an aggressive bear can do to disrupt the life of a wolf pack. It had been several years since they had seen one another, but now the dreaded bear was back in force.

Mohegan slowly crept toward Otho, baring his fangs and laying back his ears. They stood at a standoff for a while, staring at one another while Mohegan determined what to do next. Otho opened his huge mouth, baring his teeth in a show of defiance and power. Most wolves would have left and returned later to see if the bear had left any scraps. However, bears will usually guard a food source for many days and sometimes weeks. It's not uncommon for a large bear to sleep on the carcass to prevent scavenging by other animals. There was no guarantee that returning to the kill site would be productive for the wolves.

To lose a kill after an extensive chase is a great expenditure and waste of energy without a nutritional reward. This would be highly detrimental to the pack's health. It would also be bad for morale, which is vitally important, especially with a large pack such as Mohegan's. Mohegan could not allow this bear to take his pack's rightful kill. Mohegan had never faced a bear in combat before. He knew he was the only one in the pack capable of any attack on the bear. However, he didn't see any clear options that did not endanger his life.

Mohegan feigned a lunge at the big bear, making the bear swing and miss with his massive paw. Mohegan bolted around the bear, forcing Otho to turn to face him. Wachak and the other wolves took

the cue, running in circles around Otho, nipping at his rear and then quickly retreating. Soon the wolves were circling around the bear, making him turn to face them in numerous directions. Otho appeared to be spinning like a top astride the moose carcass, but he remained undeterred with his large, toothed mouth wide open. One thing wolves and bears have in common is persistence. Otho was not going away. He was willing to stay on the moose for as long as it took until the harassing wolves left. The moose carcass was too great a prize to be let go since this huge source of protein could sustain him for weeks if not months to come.

Aside from harassing the bear, the wolves didn't know what to do. Mohegan was no match for the bear because of his fearsome physical weaponry, and Otho knew this. Mohegan either had to walk away with a future of bad consequences or take a serious calculated risk to his life to attack the bear. Mohegan instinctively knew that with great responsibility comes great risk. He had to do what was best for the pack. He decided to take the risk, but it had to be done strategically. Timing and explosive power were critical.

While the wolves were rapidly circling Otho, keeping him distracted, Mohegan casually loped away as if leaving the area. When he was away from Otho's awareness, Mohegan turned and ran at top speed while the bear's back was toward him. Without breaking stride, he flew into the air with his huge fanged mouth wide open and buried his knifelike teeth deep in the rump of the big bear. The bear instantly raised his head and bellowed, a horrible sound that reverberated throughout the forest. The bite took out a large portion of muscle that would leave the bear permanently scarred. Within a split second, Mohegan took a second large bite of the bear's back.

The bear spun around with Mohegan holding his viselike jaws tight. Mohegan's body was flying around with his hind legs extended in the air beyond the bear's reach as he continued to hold on with his deeply implanted fangs. Using the bear's turning momentum, Mohegan finally released his jaws and immediately flew away from the wounded bear faster than Otho could retaliate.

This terrible injury inflicted by Mohegan struck severe pain and fear into Otho, who was now bleeding profusely. The bear bolted from the carcass as fast as he could run into the bush. The entire wolf pack chased him, harassing him for several miles. The bear was now in fear of his life, something he had never experienced before. The pack eventually broke off the chase and returned with Mohegan to the moose carcass to finish their well-earned meal.

The wolves were awestruck by their courageous alpha leader. None of the wolves had ever seen a wolf chase a large male bear from a kill site. Their respect for their leader grew even greater. Otho left the territory and was never seen there again. Mohegan was now truly the master of his domain.

The She-Wolf

Sinapu was a beautiful wolf. She had areas of snow-white fur evenly mixed with gray. She likely had some arctic wolf blood in her, as they are completely white. She never growled or snapped at other wolves. However, she had a calm dignity that the other wolves respected. When feeding at a kill, the other wolves would move away from her, letting her feed uncontested. However, she was not physically intimidating or menacing. For a female wolf, she was of average size and a slightly faster runner than most.

Mohegan had noticed her for some time and respected her. He had known her as a pup, when she was the sole survivor of the bear attack that had killed her siblings. He had spent his youth with her and considered her a close friend along with Wachak. However, she was a few years younger than he. Now, as the alpha male, Mohegan began brushing up against her and licking her face as a sign of affection. Sinapu was calm and demure in response to Mohegan's advances. They slowly began to play like puppies. Mohegan would lie on his back in front of her, kick his legs in the air, and then get up and run in a circle around Sinapu. She found it amusing that such a large and potentially dangerous wolf would act like a fun-loving young puppy. Be it wolf or man, courtship begins with acting as silly and playful as a child. This was in stark contrast to Mohegan's usual stern and serious behavior.

During the hunt, Sinapu began running next to Mohegan. He noted how swiftly she ran and her smooth and elegant stride. The way she ran was more of glide compared to the choppy up-and-down gallop of most wolves. The more he studied her, the more he liked what he saw. She exhibited her own unique leadership qualities among the pack members. The pack didn't fear her as they feared Mohegan, yet she was respected for her intelligence and good judgment. She kept up with Mohegan stride for stride for miles on end. She became like another second-in-command, similar to Wachak. She knew when to break off from the main pack while Wachak took his group away for an ambush. With three groups, the pack was able to perform even more complicated hunting strategies with maximum effectiveness. The rest of the pack looked to Sinapu and Wachak for orders as if the two were corps commanders under the main general, Mohegan. Sinapu and Wachak seemed to know exactly what Mohegan was thinking during a hunt and executed it with precision. The pack changed from a blunt-instrument type of killing machine to a precise surgical instrument, requiring far less effort and potential danger. The entire pack was in good spirits during this time because full bellies always improve morale. They grew to not only respect Sinapu but love and admire her. She became a worthy queen of her domain.

It was a longer-than-usual courtship between the two wolves, but eventually they became the new alpha wolf pair. They subsequently had three litters of pups, substantially increasing the size of the pack. Sinapu turned out to be a loving and wise mother. Before Sinapu, Mohegan had looked at the world as fierce and brutal without warmth. If ever there could be love between two animals, Mohegan and Sinapu had it. Mohegan had felt the satisfaction of kindness and caring only in the distant past. He recalled such a feeling from his parents long ago. He now received this from Sinapu and their pups. He felt that life was now complete thanks to Sinapu.

Having recently had a litter, Sinapu longed to go on the hunt with the pack. However, her strongest instinct was to stay in the den and care for her pups. She licked them from head to toe, cleaning them to prevent disease. Occasionally she walked outside the small den, which was surrounded by thick bushes and well concealed, then return to the pups, who were nursing nearly continuously. Several of the younger female wolves were stationed around the den for anything Sinapu or the pups needed and for protection from other predators.

It had been over two months since Sinapu had left the den for any length of time while nursing her litter. The pups were starting to be weaned. They were becoming more independent and venturing out of the den more often under close supervision. There were seven pups, all of whom were quite healthy from excellent nutrition and care. During play they rolled around the den site like little balls of fur. Their play mimicked ambush, chase, and attacks, which was genetically imprinted on them. Sinapu and the yearling wolves were continuously vigilant, observing the pups and keeping them out of trouble. When they strayed too far from the den site, they were herded or carried back by the nape of the neck. When the pack returned from a hunt, the pups would bolt out of the den to greet the adults. They jumped at Mohegan and the other wolves, licking their faces and wagging their tiny tails, anticipating their now preferred food, regurgitated meat, as they were weaned from their mother's milk.

After the passage of time, Sinapu returned to the hunt. When she left the den to finally rejoin the pack, she ran jubilantly around Mohegan. She playfully and flirtatiously flicked the end of her tail in his face and then turned to look at him. He gave her a look of amusement. She then jumped into the air with all four legs in an expression of excitement. He too was glad that she was back to run with the hunt. He knew the pack ran better with her along, like oil to a finely tuned motor. Upon seeing Sinapu rejoin the pack for the hunt, the entire group crowded around her and howled with excitement. She was considered a clear asset.

The pack was getting ready to follow a herd of caribou. Sinapu couldn't wait to get started and feel the exhilaration of the chase again. She placed a few segments of bone and antler in the den as toys for the pups to play with. She took one last look at her offspring and then was off with the pack. She suddenly felt an exhilaration she hadn't felt in months. As she loped along with Mohegan, she felt her stiff, unused muscles loosen with each stride. With each mile she ran, she slowly regained her strength from being inactive for so long in the den. She was beginning to feel as if she'd been reborn, doing something she was genetically programmed to do.

After several hours the pack picked up the scent of a caribou herd. The caribou trail followed the edge of a frozen lake. It was here that Sinapu sensed a subtle, distant scent of nearby meat. She broke away from the pack and climbed the bank of the frozen shoreline. There she saw something she had never seen before—a red cloth tied to a tree branch. She had no idea what this curious item was. She thought that on her return from the hunt, she would retrieve this colorful thing and bring it back to the pups as a toy. It had an unusual scent that she didn't recognize. A piece of caribou meat hung nearby on another branch. Not a huge meal, but easy pickings. She went over to the hanging meat and sniffed. Besides the scent of caribou, it had the same unfamiliar scent as the red cloth. She was unaware that there was a predator such as man and the potential danger this strange animal represented, but she was wary as she cautiously approached the beckoning tasty snack. It was too good to pass up after months in the den eating regurgitated meat brought to her by Mohegan and others. She disregarded her usual caution and the strange human scent.

Mohegan turned and looked at his mate sniffing the unusual hanging meat in the distance. He could now detect the subtle scent of man, which set off a horrible fearful alarm in him. He gave a yelp as he sped to her, urgently bounding through the snow and up the lakeshore embankment to warn her. Before Mohegan could reach her,

Sinapu jumped up and grabbed the meat. As she came down, there was a loud snap followed by a screeching yelp from Sinapu. She felt a searing pain in her leg from a steel trap.

She immediately jumped away, but her leg was stuck. Mohegan didn't know what was holding Sinapu. However, when he smelled the scent of man and witnessed the trap holding Sinapu's leg, he knew this was another of man's magical killing devices. His heart sank. He tried to bite and break the steel device. He tried pulling it away from its attachment to the tree with multiple violent yanks on the chain, but without success. He was at a loss for what to do. He began circling the tree, trying to devise a plan. The remainder of the pack had since given up following the caribou and were now surrounding Sinapu, who was softly whimpering in the blood-tinged snow.

The War

Since leaving his campsite at the farthest point in his trek four days before, Isha had been doing well on his way home. His trapline was more successful than he had ever imagined. The great majority of the furs were mink and ermine, which were the most valuable. Isha thought he had been lucky and struck the jackpot this time. Fox, marten, beaver, otter, and lynx furs were piled high in the sled as well. He already had many more furs than he had taken in the past, and he was only halfway through. He was considering making a second, smaller accessory sled to attach to and be pulled by the main sled, filling it with furs on his next stop. He was elated that he had conquered not only a new land filled with valuable furs but also his fear and made a near spiritual connection to his ancestors with the discovery of the giant black rock.

He thought, *My wife will be very pleased with me and all the extra money I'll get from these furs.* He couldn't wait to see the smile on Cici's pretty face and to see his young child again. Isha was already well respected in his village as an excellent provider and a young leader of his community. Now, with all these furs, his prestige would grow even more. If this trapline continued as it had, it would produce more fur than anyone had ever brought in. He imagined Angus's face and how proud he would be as he piled all the valuable furs on the counter at the trading post.

Isha's mood was high, and he broke out into a song. He sang several traditional Cree songs that his ancestors had passed down to celebrate hunting victory. The songs reverberated along the barren frozen lake and through the surrounding forest as if he were in a canyon hearing an echo of himself. He sang as loudly as he could, moving his body with the tune. Atu briefly looked back and sensed his master's good spirits. Isha noted Atu's glance and began to laugh. He thought he detected a big grin on Atu—that is, if dogs could grin.

"We're heading for good times, my friend," Isha said to his lead dog. He yelled to the frozen forest at the top of his lungs, "This is my land now, a land of wealth and bounty that no one dared enter. Only I was not afraid!"

As Isha steadily cruised along the frozen lakeshore while happily singing, he noted some movement in the bush just ahead on the bank of the lake where a red cloth marker was. He stopped singing and slowed the dogs to investigate further. He saw the area covered with wolf tracks that looked recent. His mood abruptly changed to one of concern. He halted the sled and ordered the dogs to stay as he grabbed his rifle. He climbed up the steep bank of the lake and began to slowly walk through the forest in a cautious bent-over position. Ahead, he saw increased activity and movement through the trees. He became acutely on guard because the number of tracks indicated a large pack. He had to see what was in the trap. He expected to see wolves eating an already trapped dead animal, as occasionally happened. Isha anticipated scaring the wolves away and then dealing with the trap. He wasn't overly fearful because he had his rifle at the ready.

As Isha stealthily walked closer to the trap, more wolves than he had ever encountered gradually came into view through the dense underbrush. This was an enormous pack by any standard. He had heard of giant packs like this only in legends. He'd never imagined the stories could be true. In the center of the pack was the largest wolf he had ever seen, so large that he wasn't sure what it was at first but thought it might be a large gray bear. On closer inspection, it was a wolf, but a giant one, nearly twice the size of a regular wolf. Its head was uncharacteristically large and broad. A regular wolf's head was narrower and more pointed. The giant wolf's face was more bearlike than wolflike; nevertheless, it was truly a wolf. Isha remembered old stories of giant wolves that had lived in ancient days. He became concerned that the wolves didn't flee at the sight of him, as he would have expected.

Isha then saw a wolf that was partly white still very much alive, caught in his trap and struggling frantically. This trapped wolf was pulling at the chain with hard jerking but ineffective movements. Isha raised his gun toward the sky and fired. The wolf pack scattered, but not very far. The big wolf jumped away behind some nearby trees as soon as Isha raised his gun and before he had fired, as if the big wolf knew what the gun could do.

Mohegan was filled with dread. He remembered the magical stick with which a man had killed his father long ago. Now he saw it again in the hands of this man approaching his mate.

Isha walked over to the trapped wolf. It was impossible for him to release her without being bitten and seriously damaged. He shook his head with regret.

Mohegan knew that if he attacked the man, he would be killed as his father had been. All he could do was watch the man's every movement and hopefully wait for a mistake that would make him vulnerable.

Isha knew what had to be done, and he hated it. With a pang of regret, he took aim at the trapped wolf's heart and fired.

The other wolves scattered again. He unhooked the steel trap and threw it over his shoulder. He wasn't about to rebait the trap or even take the wolf carcass away in the present situation, surrounded by an angry pack. He just wanted to get his trap and get out of there in one piece as quickly as possible.

Mohegan and the pack looked on in horror. Except for Mohegan, the wolves had never before seen a man or heard the loud noise of his magic stick. Little did Isha know that his action would set in motion a lifetime of irrevocable consequences for him and the wolves.

Isha saw the giant wolf come out from behind the trees, staring at him. Isha didn't see the slightest fear in the wolf, only tremendous anger and hate. The fur on the back of the giant wolf bristled. His huge teeth were showing, exposing large canine fangs. The wolf was otherwise silent, standing his ground and continuing to glare at Isha.

Isha slowly walked backward toward the frozen lake with his rifle at the ready, not daring to turn his back on the giant wolf. Carefully he slid down the embankment on his side and onto the snow-covered frozen surface.

Looking back, he saw a long line of wolves on the embankment overlooking the frozen lake, staring at him with no sign of fear. These wolves were different than most. They all appeared to be large, healthy, and particularly dangerous. He had never sensed emotion from animals before, but now he felt the overwhelming sense of raging hatred. Isha could feel the tension building between him and the wolves.

He walked toward the dog sled, keeping his eyes on the glowering wolves and his rifle ready. He knew that if he ran, it would trigger an attack from these deadly predators, who would overtake him in no time. Mohegan barked and yelped at his pack mates, telling them not to attack the man but to come to the alpha wolf. However, they seemed oblivious to his commands, as if blinded by anger. Mohegan had long ago seen how dangerous man could be, and he knew he had to be cautious despite the overwhelming urge to attack and set his rage loose. He knew he had to wait or he and his pack would come to the same fate as Sinapu.

Isha was now about fifty yards away from the wolves and close to the sled. He could tell that the dogs were frightened and anxious. They were nervously glancing at the menacing wolves, but they were staying put as their master had ordered. The dogs cast fleeting glances back toward Isha, anticipating the order to get up and run quickly. He reassured the terrified dogs by saying in a low, calm voice, "Whoa now, whoa now, settle down, everything is going to be fine."

Suddenly the pent-up rage and emotion of the pack erupted. The wolves flooded over the embankment like a dam bursting, charging Isha and the dogs. Mohegan held back and barked at them to stop. In the heat of the moment, the pack ignored the giant wolf and charged the killer of their beloved alpha she-wolf, determined to tear the man and his dogs to pieces. Over twenty wolves charged Isha with a single-minded wish to kill.

Isha quickly raised his gun to his shoulder, calmly took aim at the closest wolf, and fired. He then engaged his lever-action rifle within a split second and

fired again,

then again,

then again,

then again.

Several wolves fell sprawling on the snow, yelping in pain, and the pack dispersed and ran back into the brush, leaving five dead wolves behind. Isha's actions were an amazing display of coolness under fire and superb marksmanship.

Isha got on the sled and loudly yelled, "MUSH!" The dogs bolted out like a rocket. Isha momentarily felt invincible and proud of his shooting accuracy under pressure.

With their heads bowed and tails between their legs in a sign of submission, the remaining wolves gathered around Mohegan. Wachak nipped and growled at them for disobeying Mohegan's orders. This was the first time the wolf pack hadn't followed Mohegan's commands, and they had paid a bitter price by losing five of their valuable comrades. They were now fully aware of what a man's magic killing devices could do. Mohegan knew it would take stealth and cunning to bring down the ultimate predator, man. He would turn all his energy, focus, and strategy from hunting to revenge against the man.

To Mohegan, the killing of Sinapu seemed senseless and without reason. He felt that man was an evil presence on the earth who had killed his father and now his mate. Mohegan had never felt such rage in his life, but he controlled his feelings so that he could exact revenge on the man more effectively. He determined that his blood vendetta will be fulfilled: this was war.

After traveling a considerable distance, Isha looked back and saw no wolves. He thought the wolves had learned their lesson and would probably not return. He breathed a deep sigh of relief and slowed the dogs to a steady trot. He then recalled the terrible dream he'd had nearly a year before, when he had passed by a dead, nearly all-white wolf, shot in the chest, strangely reminiscent of the wolf he had just killed in the trap. He immediately put the terrible dream out of his mind and concentrated on the business at hand.

After thirty minutes had passed, he saw one of his red markers. He stopped the sled and walked into the bush where the trap was. The trap had been sprung, but the animal had been taken by a predator. This occasionally happened, but when he looked around at the snow, he was alarmed. The area was covered with wolf tracks. He noted that one paw print was huge. The giant wolf had gotten there with his pack before Isha had. He quickly looked around but didn't see anything. He stood silent and didn't hear a sound except the wind through the trees.

Isha went on. The next several sets of traps were all sprung and the trapped animals taken, just as before. Again wolf tracks were everywhere, including the tracks of the big one. These were not random events but a planned course of action taken by the wolves to follow his trapline and deprive him of his fur. He realized that this was no ordinary wolf. He had made a deadly and determined enemy.

The warning given by Tiskigapon several weeks earlier had become a reality. He was being stalked like a game animal. This had the signs of intelligent planning. He was now in the unenviable position of having to react to whatever the wolves were planning. He was at a disadvantage but had no choice. He wondered what would come next.

Isha decided not to rebait and reset the traps. He had more than enough furs and was willing to let well enough alone and pick up the remaining traps for another trip. He had a deep feeling that he was being watched, but as he looked around, he saw no wolves. It was now approaching dusk, and he planned to make camp soon. The next shelter that he had built on his way up came into view.

Isha heard the howl of a wolf close to where he planned to camp. He stopped for a moment to observe. Another long, haunting howl came from his right in the forest, then another across the frozen lake to his left. Then a whole chorus of wolves began howling together from all directions. He was surrounded! Fear ran through his body. He felt a flush of perspiration as his heart raced. He grabbed his gun and looked in all directions but saw nothing.

"No!" he yelled out loud. "I am not afraid! I will fight you!"

His voice carried across the frozen lake and into the brush, temporarily halting the howling. Isha knew that fear was deadly and could sap his strength and diminish his will to resist. He couldn't allow that to happen. He had to control his mind and his emotions to stay alive. The dogs' ears perked up, and they began turning their heads in nervous anxiety. Isha talked to the dogs to calm them: "We'll be just fine, boys. Don't mind that racket. We'll be at camp soon and have some dinner. That will make all of you happy." The dogs' ears went down with Isha's reassurance. They continued to do their duty pulling the sled.

While Isha spoke to the dogs, he began formulating a plan to set an ambush at the campsite. He felt certain that the wolves would visit him that night. He would go on the offensive. He would not let things happen to him. He thought, *After all, I am a great Cree hunter!* He grasped his medicine pouch. The sudden rush of fear was now gone as he reminded himself who he was and remembered his ability. He recalled that he had already killed five wolves. The thought of this small victory gave him some solace. His moment of doubt was now gone.

As he came closer to the camp, the chorus of howling wolves resumed. Isha responded by yelling at the top of his voice, "Aaaaaaahhhhhh!" This time the howling continued unabated and seemed so close that he didn't understand why he couldn't see the wolves. The barking sounds varied in intensity. Isha thought the giant wolf was somehow giving orders for a plan of attack. It came to Isha that this giant wolf was a smart one. Unique, much different from a usual wolf.

Isha pulled off the frozen lake and parked the sled close to the shelter. He put the canvas over the wooden structure and staked it to the frozen ground. He unhooked the dogs from their harnesses and fed them some caribou meat and pemmican. He kept working as the wolves continued to howl.

He bedded the dogs down under a spruce tree with long, low-hanging branches. They were nervous because of the wolves' nonstop howling. Their ears were up as they anxiously moved their heads in all directions, fidgeting with their closely packed bodies. Isha knew that howling was part of the wolves' strategy to create fear and panic in their prey so it would lose concentration and make mistakes. Isha was determined to disregard it. He made two fires, one in the shelter and one outside near the dogs. He grabbed two bars of pemmican and quickly ate them. He then reassessed the topography of the area. *Yes, the perfect spot for an ambush!* A spruce with a large trunk and thick branches overlooked the dogs and the campsite.

Isha climbed the tree, rifle in hand. He found a sturdy branch to sit on and another on which to rest his rifle. He then settled in. He had a clear view of the entire area as well as the cluster of dogs. Darkness slowly enveloped the camp. After he situated himself in the tree, the howling finally stopped.

Several hours passed, and Isha was still on high alert, expecting the wolves at any time. He knew they would come, but they were certainly taking their time. Then he noted a subtle sound of scurrying through the brush. He aimed his rifle in the direction of the sound and thought, *Okay, giant wolf, just poke your head out and your head will be gone.* He heard the muffled sound again, rustling through the underbrush. The sound would start, quickly stop, and then start again.

He placed his finger softly on the trigger of his rifle but detected no obvious movement. He waited patiently, peering down the gunsight of the rifle. If the sounds weren't from a stealthy wolf, then he had no idea what they were. Suddenly a pine squirrel hopped into the clearing of the camp. He watched as the squirrel skittered around the area looking for food. Then he heard another soft, muffled sound, much different than the previous sound. Whatever was making this sound was hurtling rapidly through the trees. A large snowy owl came rocketing into the campsite and pounced on the unsuspecting squirrel. Isha took a deep breath and sighed softly. He slightly changed his uncomfortable position. His anxiety diminished. He occasionally heard the wind whistling through the forest, followed by the thuds of built-up snow falling to the ground from branches.

More hours passed with no sign of the wolves. The weather was turning even colder. It was now 10 degrees below zero Fahrenheit. Isha was become more uncomfortable sitting motionless in the tree. He wanted to move but didn't dare give away his ambush position. He began to shiver. He tried to stop, but it was uncontrollable. He needed to stay quiet and motionless.

The fire near the dogs was now reduced to glowing orange embers. He wondered what the wolves were up to. He wanted to do something unexpected to surprise them and regain the initiative instead of waiting for the wolves to do something to him. However, he knew a successful hunter needed to be patient.

He thought of Cici and his young son in their warm cabin. They would both be bedded down by now, cozy and comfortable under thick fur blankets in front of a glowing fire. He'd give anything to be home. He then recalled the wolves he'd seen on the tribal caribou hunt and the dream he'd had the night before the trek. He was now convinced that these dreams were omens. He realized one should never take the spirit world lightly and ignore its messages. But he still wasn't sure what message the Great Spirit was trying to convey. He did know that Tiskigapon had warned him about making a determined enemy of wolves, but there was nothing he could do about that now.

Along with being terribly uncomfortable, he was getting sleepy. His mind began to lose focus and drift away to random thoughts. He fought the wandering of his mind with a renewed concentration. His eyes closed and his head dropped. Isha caught himself, and his eyes snapped open. He tried to judge whether he'd been asleep or simply dozing. He thought most likely the latter. He shook his head and yawned.

Out of the corner of his eye he saw something move, so slowly that it could easily have been overlooked. Several minutes passed. The camp was eerily quiet. He began to doubt whether he'd really seen anything. Maybe he was seeing things because of anticipation and wishful thinking. The subtle movement stopped as he stared at the place where he thought it had been. *It's probably nothing, maybe another squirrel or some other animal. Probably a porcupine,* he told himself. *They're slow and can make a subtle noise as they chew tree bark.* The north woods were filled with nocturnal animals looking for food.

Just when he began to discount the supposed movement, another area of irregularity in the brush caught his eye, then another, until suddenly the entire wolf pack was at the forest edge, peering into the campsite. They appeared as indistinct shadows but definitely wolves. He could see a multitude of glaring yellow eyes in the dark, just waiting. For what, he didn't know. Isha knew that just shooting a few more wolves wouldn't solve his problem. He knew he had to kill the giant wolf, or the stalking would continue. Isha carefully took off his mittens and aimed his rifle in the direction of the wolves.

The night was black with heavy cloud cover and no moon. He could barely see the wolves' outlines, like shadows within darkness. But he knew there were a lot of them. The yellow eyes were everywhere in the brush beyond the campsite. They just stood there watching, nearly surrounding the campsite.

Isha didn't have a clear shot, but he remained patient. His fingers were starting to become numb from the cold, but he put discomfort out of his mind. He was concentrating on the wolves' next move. If they came only a few feet closer, he would have a good shot. What he really wanted was to see the giant wolf and kill him, but if not, then any wolf would do for the time being. He still couldn't fathom why they were just standing there without moving. However, when they did move in, he would be ready to give them a painful surprise.

Out of the corner of his eye Isha saw the giant wolf come into full view away from the main group of wolves. It was stealthily sniffing around the entrance of the shelter. Isha pivoted the rifle, aiming at him. Just as he was ready to fire, the wolf quickly moved behind the shelter out of view. Isha knew that if he could kill the giant wolf, this terrible ordeal would be over. He aimed his rifle at the other end of the shelter, where he thought the animal would next emerge. All this time the other wolves maintained their position just inside the edge of the dense forest.

He waited, ready to pull the trigger the second the giant wolf showed his huge head. He had hunted other prey thousands of times before by waiting for an animal to emerge from a protected spot and show itself. He just needed to see that big head peer out from behind the shelter. He was pointing the rifle at just the right level of the wolf's height.

He waited.

He waited.

He waited.

Isha had the odd sensation that he was being watched. He had felt this sensation many times before and knew that he should trust his intuition. He heard a slight movement just below the tree where he was perched. He quickly looked down and saw the glaring yellow eyes of the giant wolf looking at him coldly and calculatedly, as if trying to analyze this man in the tree. Isha felt that in some deeply disturbing way, this wolf was trying to communicate with him. The giant wolf didn't growl or bare his fangs. Isha could detect a deep, malignant hatred but also keen intelligence behind those glaring eyes. The giant wolf seemed to be saying, *Our business is not finished yet. You can't outsmart me. You will never return to your village!* Isha had the horrible sensation that he was a prey animal, like a rabbit being stalked by something vicious that would devour him.

Because Isha was taken off guard by the giant wolf, he uncharacteristically hesitated to bring his rifle to bear on it while the two adversaries stared at one another. It was as if the giant wolf had placed a temporary spell on Isha. What was less than a few seconds seemed like thirty minutes.

By the time he swung his rifle around to aim, the giant wolf had bolted out of view into the darkness. Isha looked up and noticed that the other wolves were gone. He took his finger off the trigger and lightly banged his forehead on the tree branch in frustration. He angrily thought, *I could've shot the giant wolf when he was below me if only I had been more alert. This whole terrible affair could've been over!* Isha raised his head, took a deep breath, and sighed. He was amazed at how the giant wolf had sneaked around the shelter and come under the tree without him noticing. *Why did he bother to come under the tree to glare at me when he knew I was ready for an ambush un-*

less he wanted to convey some message? What kind of animal would do such a thing?

Isha stayed in the tree for another hour, but he knew the wolves weren't coming back. By the time he climbed down, the sun was starting to rise. He walked to the sled and grabbed several bars of pemmican for himself and the dogs. He rekindled the fire to warm his stiff, frozen body after the miserable night in the tree. He stretched his aching muscles. He made some strong coffee and thought about his next move. He knew his ordeal with the wolves was not over but in fact was just beginning.

Isha realized that when the giant wolf had stealthily entered the camp and sniffed the shelter entrance, he had understood that Isha was not inside, which had set off an alarm in the giant wolf. The wolf's extraordinary sense of smell then told him where Isha was hiding. Like the wise and careful leader he was, the giant wolf had the pack wait just out of rifle range until he could determine the situation and find where the man was waiting. Isha thought, *This wolf is very clever. He came over to let me know he knew exactly what I was doing and that he wasn't outsmarted. He played the situation perfectly. He did this to further unsettle me.*

Isha broke camp, hooked the dogs to the sled harnesses, and was off again. After an hour of cold silence gliding over the snow of the frozen lake, he began to hear howling again in all directions. As Isha continued toward his next camp, he intermittently heard the wolves throughout the day. The howls kept pace with him as he progressed down the frozen lake. He saw many of his red pieces of cloth tied to branches, but now he simply drove past them. He realized that stopping would be futile and would put him in danger of an ambush by the stalking wolf pack, which now seemed to be even closer. He occasionally caught fleeting glimpses of movement in the forest, like ghosts darting through the brush. Isha had the sensation that they were closing in even though he couldn't always see them.

Isha understood that his greatest vulnerability was at night, when his vision was poor, while the wolves had excellent night vision. He dreaded the coming of night. The giant wolf seemed to know this human vulnerability and would exploit this advantage. Isha was greatly fatigued and desperately needed sleep.

It was close to evening by the time he neared the next shelter, where he had planned to stay the night. Before turning off to his campsite, he looked back toward the lake. He saw five wolves less than a mile away, loping toward him. To his side above the bank of the lake, he noticed movement in the brush and saw several wolves staring at him. Isha knew what they were doing. They wanted him to see them. He thought, *These wolves are smart; they're playing psychological warfare with me, wanting me to panic, to slowly break down my spirit and will to survive.* Isha had no option but to stay in the shelter overnight since his village was still far away.

Isha quickly gathered as much firewood as possible before the sun set. He built several tall stacks of dead wood around the camp, making bonfires that he hoped would burn all night and deter the wolves from drawing too close. He knew the wolves were near, but none were in sight. At least they had stopped howling. He placed the canvas over the lashed-together wooden poles and reinforced the canvas tepee with large stakes that he pounded into the ground around the perimeter, hoping the stakes would prevent any wolf from sliding in under the edge. The spruce and pine boughs were still inside the shelter from when Isha had last used it. He knew this kind of shelter would be totally inadequate protection against a large bear attack, and he wondered how it would fare in the face of an attack by a determined wolf pack. Isha was three to four nights away from his village and safety. He worried about what the next several days would bring.

The sun set, sending the camp into darkness. Isha lit the stacks of wood in a circle around the camp, making large bonfires, including one close to the dogs. The fires lit up the entire area. He fed the dogs and cooked himself some caribou meat and hot tea. He entered his shelter and placed the musk ox blanket over him. He felt snug and warm. It had been a long, stressful day. He hadn't slept in over twenty-four hours. He was looking forward to a good night's sleep.

Just as he was dozing off into deep sleep, comfortable in his small shelter, he heard the howl of a wolf nearby. Then he heard another, followed by another, and then a cacophony of howling in all directions. This sent a combined sensation of fear and anger through Isha. He got up, flung open the canvas door flap, and looked around. He didn't see anything out of the ordinary. The fires were still going, but with less intensity. He could tell that the dogs were anxious, huddled together like one large ball of fur. Isha put on his mukluks, grabbed his rifle, and went outside. He could hear rustling and movement in the brush. As he looked more closely, he spotted several eyes peering at him from the and reflecting the light of the fires. Amid the continuous howling, he grabbed a piece of burning wood and threw it into the dark forest in the direction of the glaring eyes, at the same time yelling, "GET OUT OF HERE!" He then fired a round from his rifle blindly into the brush. All went silent.

He could do no more. Unfortunately, the pine and birchwood

burned relatively quickly. Foraging for more firewood beyond the perimeter of the camp would leave him vulnerable in the dark forest. He knew he had to get some sleep to be effective the next day. He walked to the dogs and gathered them all around him. He hugged and rubbed them within a big huddle. He said reassuringly, "Don't be scared, fellas. We'll all get home safe and sound. I'll take good care of you." The dogs looked up at him, happy with their master's reassuring presence and comforting words.

He went to Atu and said, "Look after your friends tonight, big fellow." He rubbed Atu's head and belly. Atu seemed to appreciate the attention because he was fearful, like the other dogs. The dogs were right to fear their natural enemy, the wolf. Even the strongest dog is no match for a wolf, let alone an entire pack. Isha got up and went back into the tepee. He kept his mukluks on in case he had to get up quickly during the night. He put a few more logs on the fire within his shelter, closed his eyes, and fell asleep.

The next thing Isha knew, he was being dragged out of his shelter by his feet. He was surrounded by the entire wolf pack, and the giant wolf was staring at him inches from his face, snarling with bared fangs. Isha fought back, throwing kicks and punches. His efforts were like mere whispers against the wolves' strength. Isha was in a panic, moving his head rapidly from side to side and trying to yell for help, but no sound came from his mouth.

Isha woke from his dream with a jolt, screaming as he sat up in a cold sweat. He took a few deep breaths and thought, *What a terrible nightmare. At least this time I wasn't killed.* He realized that he had been asleep for just a few minutes when he'd had the nightmare. He had barely dozed off. He knew he had to get some sleep. He lay back down, still heavily breathing, staring at the top of the shelter with his eyes wide open. He pulled the musk ox blanket over him and tried to go back to sleep.

The large bonfires were now beds of glowing coals. Atu slowly awakened and felt that something was not right. He poked his head up above the other huddled dogs. He couldn't see anything in the dark of the early-morning hours.

Out of nowhere and without warning, a huge wolf flew at Nicimos. It was so sudden and violent that the dogs didn't have time to bark. Within seconds Mohegan had placed his huge open mouth around the dog's neck, clamped down, and with one powerful shake of his head torn away the tissue of the neck, instantly killing poor Nicimos. At the same time two wolves darted in low from the opposite direction and lunged at Jabweh's leg but missed. The dog jumped up on his hind legs in a defensive maneuver and turned to face his attackers, exposing his torso and abdomen. From another direction, Wachak and another wolf grabbed Jabweh's abdomen on both sides and fiercely bit into the deep internal tissues. The wolves then vanished into the darkness as quickly as they had appeared, leaving the remaining dogs in shock.

The wolves must have run at the group of dogs in a coordinated manner and then jumped in the air at them in unison, since they had seemed to suddenly appear out of nowhere, catching the dogs off guard and unaware. The wolves were smart enough to begin their attack downwind so that the dogs couldn't sense the impending attack. The wolves were skilled killers who knew their craft well.

The sudden attack left Nicimos dead and Jabweh severely injured, lying on his side panting in a large pool of blood. There had been no growling, no barking, no dogfight. It had been a perfectly planned assassination carried out with vicious effectiveness, a classic hit-and-run guerrilla attack.

Mohegan had carefully assessed the group of dogs before the attack and determined which were the most vulnerable. Nicimos and Jabweh were the youngest and smallest of the group and thus the first to be attacked. This was something the wolf pack understood well. Their routine when hunting caribou was to isolate the weak animals from the rest of the herd and then bring them down. The wolves' instinct was to kill all the dogs at once and to eat their fallen prey, as they had done to Talgu's invading wolf pack, since they greatly outnumbered the dogs and were much stronger. However, this would have taken more time, leaving them vulnerable to the man's retribution with his deadly magic stick. Mohegan's imposed discipline was proving stronger than the wolf pack's instinct.

Only after the attack did the stunned group of dogs began to bark and yelp. On hearing the dogs in distress, Isha bolted out from beneath his blanket and ran outside with his gun. He then witnessed the carnage.

He knelt to inspect the dogs and softly touched their bodies. He placed his hands on them and lamented out loud, "Oh, my Nicimos and Jabweh, both of you were the fastest and the happiest of all. I will miss you so." Jabweh was still alive but severely injured.

As Isha inspected the two dogs, he was amazed at how much of the neck had been torn from Nicimos and how little other damage there was. Jabweh had deep gashes on each side of his abdomen, implying internal injuries and possibly bleeding. Isha stroked Jabweh, trying to comfort the injured dog. Victims of a wolf attack usually had extensive multiple injuries and were torn apart. He realized the wisdom of the wolf's plan: this had been a quick, surgical strike.

He looked around and saw and heard nothing except the soft whimpering of the unnerved remaining dogs. He felt helpless and angry. There was nothing he could do. There was no way he could go back to sleep, so he placed a few more nearby sticks on the glowing embers. He sat by the fire with his rifle on his lap, close to the traumatized dogs, stroking Jabweh.

Just before dawn, Isha fed the dogs and had a quick breakfast of pemmican and coffee. Jabweh was unable to stand or eat and would clearly not be able to pull the sled. At least Jabweh had made it through the night. Isha looked around and saw no evidence of the wolves. He knew dogs were tough and could sustain terrible injuries far more extensive than humans could tolerate and survive. He hated to leave Jabweh behind for the wolves, but he didn't have much room in the sled filled with furs. He decided to give the injured dog a chance for survival, so he removed some of the furs to make room for Jabweh.

He then broke camp, hooked the five remaining dogs into the harnesses, and went on his way across the frozen lake. Within an hour, to his right, he glimpsed wolves running through the forest. He looked back and noted several wolves a half mile behind him. He looked to his left and again noted a group of wolves near the middle of the frozen lake, more than a half mile away. They all stayed just out of range of his rifle.

He stopped the sled and grabbed his gun. He placed it on his shoulder and aimed it at the wolves behind him, hoping they would come into range as they loped toward him. As soon as he stopped the sled, however, the wolves stopped as well. They seemed to know how to stay just out of rifle range. He looked to the left and noted that the wolves in the middle of the frozen lake had stopped as well. The wolves sat and stared at Isha without movement or sound. He thought, *These are disciplined and smart wolves. They're just biding their time for an opportunity to kill me. They seem to know what my gun can do.*

Isha realized that this trapping expedition was no longer about getting furs. It was now about his survival. He already had many furs, more than he had ever trapped in the past. The main goal now was to get home alive and in one piece. He gave the command "MUSH!" and the sled was off again.

The five remaining dogs adapted well to pulling a heavier load without much reduction in speed. Angus's prediction of one dog on this special team being as strong as two from any other team had come true. Five ordinary sled dogs would have had great difficulty pulling Isha's heavily laden sled. The extra training and preparation of the dogs was paying off.

After several hours Isha noted that Jabweh had stopped breathing. He cradled the dog in his arms and placed him on the snow. He patted his lifeless head one last time, fleetingly thinking about how he would miss the fun-loving, happy-go-lucky nature of Nicimos and Jabweh. But he couldn't allow these dark thoughts to diminish the positive attitude that was essential for his survival.

Isha looked back and then to his left and noticed that the wolves were running again, keeping pace with his sled. The wolves were now continually present, always within sight. They were getting bolder and slowly closing in. They were persistently with him nearly all day. He thought, *Maybe they look at me and the dogs as a delayed meal soon to be eaten.*

After several hours with the wolves still at a distance, Isha felt a sudden dramatic drop in temperature along with a strong wind from the north. He looked at the sky, noting that the entire northern horizon was black. He knew this meant an arctic blizzard was coming quickly, and it looked like a bad one. Unless he got to shelter soon, the environment could be as deadly as the wolves. With wind chill, temperatures during an arctic blizzard could reach 100 degrees below zero Fahrenheit.

The menacing black clouds covered the horizon like a huge tidal wave rapidly approaching a tiny boat on the ocean. Isha looked back again and saw the black clouds reaching higher in the sky and moving fast. He'd never seen a blizzard come on so rapidly, seemingly whipped out of nothing. The sky had been clear that morning, with no signs of an impending change in the weather.

He yelled, "MUSH, MUSH, MUSH, YAW!" The dogs picked up the pace to an all-out run. He was trying to outrun the storm, although he knew it would be futile. The wolves were still relentlessly following, seemingly unfazed by the oncoming storm. He knew they were far better adapted to bad weather conditions than he was. Freezing temperatures had minimal effect on them. They could continue a hunt in the face of a blizzard without great difficulty.

Suddenly everything turned black, as if a giant blanket had been thrown over the world, causing a premature night. He moved the sled closer to the bank of the lake, hoping he wouldn't inadvertently fly past the shelter. Snow began to fall, pelting and stinging his face along with the wind. His cheeks and nose were becoming numb, so he bent his head to avoid full exposure. His vision was greatly diminished, not only from the dark but also because the air was so thick with snowflakes. Conditions had deteriorated so much that he couldn't see Atu at the head of the dog team. It was as if he were looking through a couple of lace veils placed over his face in the dark.

Isha looked around quickly but was unable to see the wolves. He started hearing repetitive loping footsteps. He turned around but saw only the white snow of the blizzard. He wondered if the sounds were from his own dog team and surmised that he might be becoming paranoid. However, he couldn't rule out the possibility that the wolves were just a few feet away.

He began thinking that if he were the giant wolf, he would attack now, not realizing that organizing a combined attack and changing the giant wolf's plans with the rest of the pack was difficult, if not impossible, during a blizzard when the wolves couldn't see each other or their prey. The wolves' sense of smell was also greatly diminished because of the wind and snow.

Isha knew he needed to reach the shelter soon, not only because of the wolves but to escape the frigid, life-threatening temperature. The cold penetrated his body, almost as if he were wearing no winter clothes. His teeth began to chatter. It started as a shiver along the jaw as he sucked air between his clenched teeth, but soon his whole body shook and his very bones seemed to clatter. He knew all too well that this was the first stage of hypothermia. His face was stinging and his nose felt as if it were about to fall off. Each breath he took was painful because of the frigid air entering his lungs.

Arctic blizzards were extremely dangerous for the Indigenous people who lived in the far north. Even a short exposure of the skin to such low temperatures could result in frostbite. Being caught unprepared and without shelter in an arctic blizzard was one of the leading causes of death among trappers and hunters of the tribe. Now Isha was being threatened by both the wolves and the blizzard.

Isha knew the storm would get much worse in the coming hours. There were only five hours of daylight at this time of year. When night did fall, the temperature would drop even further. He desperately needed to reach his next shelter. On the other hand, he dreaded the coming night with the ever-present wolves and what they might have instore for him. He kept going with no shelter in sight, thinking, *Where is the shelter? I need to find it soon or I'll die! Could I have unknowingly passed it already? I can't see a thing!* Minutes seemed like hours as the dogs continued to run at full speed. If he did pass the shelter, he would have to turn and face the wolves head-on in close quarters. If he had passed the shelter already and kept going, he would certainly die of exposure.

Soon he saw the vague outline of the tepee-type shelter close to the bank. "Thank God!" he said out loud. By the time he arrived at his shelter, the weather had turned into a full blizzard with blowing snow and 90 degrees below zero Fahrenheit. There was no way he could build fires to repel the wolves in this weather. He wondered if he would be harassed by wolves during the blizzard. He couldn't afford to lose any more of his dog team. To attempt to walk back to the village without the dog sled would mean certain death. His well-being was dependent on the safety of the dogs.

He took the canvas from the sled and draped it around the shelter frame. Every move he made took triple the usual effort because of his continual shivering. Tying rope to the canvas was nearly impossible, not only because it was difficult to move his hands but because he had to remove his gloves to tie the knots, causing his hands to go numb. Snow was embedded in the creases of his pants and coat, and the drifted snow was nearly up to his knees. The wind was blowing the snow in whirls, slapping Isha in the face like a cold open hand. The branches of the surrounding trees waved as if they were dreadfully alive, reaching out like grasping claws. He quickly unharnessed the dogs and fed them some pemmican. He took a frozen hard brick of pemmican and began to gnaw away, one small piece at a time. He hoped the storm would deter the wolves from attacking, but he wouldn't bet on it.

He decided to bring all five dogs into the shelter for their protection even though it was barely large enough to accommodate one person comfortably, let alone five large dogs. He was desperately tired. It had been nearly forty-eight hours since he'd had any significant sleep. He knew sleep would be difficult with the dogs in the shelter with him, but he needed them to stay alive for his own survival.

Because of the extremely cramped quarters, there was no room for a fire. The dogs were lying over one another and on Isha. Despite all the dogs' bodies, it was unbearably cold. Snow drifted in from the open area above, where smoke would normally pass out of the tepee. Isha placed the musk ox blanket over himself and the dogs. The situation would not have been too bad if he'd had a fire going inside the shelter. He would just have to suffer through the night being terribly uncomfortable and cold. The dogs, like Isha, were miserable. None of them could find a position where they could curl up without another dog lying on them or poking a paw in their face. They were so crowded together that it was difficult to breathe. The dogs were staying in place only because of the constant commands given by Isha.

The wind was blowing hard, making the canvas cover ripple like waves in an ocean storm. The wind howled more loudly than the wolves had. Despite shaking violently, it seemed that the shelter would hold up against the fierce wind, at least for the time being. Isha was glad that that he had taken the care to build the structure correctly on his way up. He had camped many times, but never in such bad conditions.

After several more terribly cold and crowded sleepless hours, he noticed that the wind had decreased dramatically. Then it stopped as quickly as it had begun. Isha gave a sigh of relief, hoping that the temperature would begin to rise and he would begin to feel somewhat more comfortable and stop shivering.

It was then that he heard digging and scratching at multiple points along the edge of the tepee. The wolves were all around the shelter, trying to get in. He knew wolves with their strength and sharp claws excelled at digging out prey from burrows and digging a den that could hold a female and her cubs within minutes. He heard the canvas being torn and ripped apart, along with a continuous low-level growling by many wolves in unison, reminding him of the rumble of thunder in the distance. Isha grabbed his rifle and cocked the lever, placing a shell in the chamber ready to fire as soon as he saw the first head of an intruding wolf slip under the tepee and expose itself. He quickly began pointing in one direction and then another, changing his aim to various locations depending on the sounds. He found it hard to hold his rifle steady because his shivering was nearly convulsive. The barrel of the rifle bobbed up and down with each involuntary movement, making it nearly impossible to aim accurately at the target. However, he was only a few feet from the digging paws, so despite his shaking, he was confident that he could place the rifle close enough to not miss. Touching the cold steel of the rifle with his bare hands caused a numbing discomfort, but like the experienced hunter he was, he ignored the pain.

Isha knew it was only a matter of time before the entire pack would crawl under the shelter. He figured that he could kill at least five or six of the wolves before he was overwhelmed. He was surprised that the giant wolf would sacrifice more wolves to get him since he had already dispatched five of their kind in their first encounter. He became resigned to his fate, ready to meet the Great Spirit. He thought, *If I am to die, I will go down fighting with honor, like a brave Cree warrior!* He began singing his death song, which all hunters of his village knew. Each song was unique to the individual. It was formulated to draw the hunter closer to the Great Spirit and dispel fear before seeing him.

The dogs were whining and squirming with fear when they saw the digging paws and heard the constant bloodcurdling growls of their mortal enemies just a few feet away. They were jumping over one another, terrified, trying to get away from the edges of the shelter. Isha was in the middle of a seething mass of fur and anxiety despite his commands to settle down and stay.

He began to see the paws of the wolves digging furiously in the frozen ground, slowly coming under the edges of the shelter. He remained vigilant, still singing and violently shaking from the cold. This went on for over an hour. He knew the cold, the violent shivering, and the anxiety were sapping his strength and energy.

Then the digging slowed dramatically. The frenzied activity was reduced to a mild pawing of the ground. The wolves could have dug under the shelter long ago if they had really wished to. He wondered why they were now taking their time. He thought maybe the digging was merely a ploy to instill fear. He knew that wolves did many things to heighten panic in their prey. Maybe this was one of their tactics.

The digging and growling around the shelter suddenly stopped. He then heard a dramatic increase in commotion in front of the tepee by the sled with his supplies. He knew the wolves were around the shelter, but this was significant. He moved some of the dogs out of the way to get to the entrance. He flung the door flap open and immediately took aim, still violently shaking. Although the wind was minimal, it was still snowing heavily, creating poor visibility in the dark. He saw several wolves scatter in the darkness. However, he saw others as vague silhouettes on top of the sled, rapidly and fiercely tearing and pulling at things.

Isha took aim in the general direction of the shadowy targets, still shaking. He fired two shots in rapid succession. He had no clear shot, but he hoped to at least scare the wolves away and maybe get lucky and hit one.

The sound of the gun firing within the small, enclosed shelter was sudden and explosively loud. Isha fired the gun inches from Tipiskaw's face. This induced immediate panic in one of his most reliable dogs. Tipiskaw was already terribly uncomfortable and anxious. The dog squirmed, jumped away from the others, and bolted past Isha out of the tepee and into the dark, snowy night. Poslite reacted to the explosive sound of the gun as well, jumping over the mound of dogs to follow his running mate out in a mindless reflex. Isha called the dogs to return, but to no avail. Within a few minutes he heard two simultaneous yelps followed by total silence. Isha called again and again. All was silent except for the muffled sound of snow falling softly on the shelter.

Isha felt the helpless sensation of dread. He thought of his pregnant wife and young child back home in the village, living a hard life without him. He wondered who would take care of them if he were gone. He thought, *My three-year-old son and my newborn will never know me.* The thought filled his soul with despair. He didn't want to die like this, being torn apart piece by piece in a slow, agonizing torture and then eaten so that nothing was left of him. Isha realized that it was the death of the she-wolf that was the cause of all this trouble and that the she-wolf had probably been the giant wolf's mate. He thought that he would probably do the same thing as the giant wolf under similar circumstances. Isha came to a grudging, fearful respect for the giant wolf.

Isha knew that the darkest thoughts usually came in the dead of night before dawn. He prayed to the Great Spirit, the maker of all things, to save him. He concluded his prayer in Jesus's name and then made the sign of the cross over his chest. He pulled his colorful beaded leather medicine pouch out of his shirt and clutched it tightly in his hand. He held it against his forehead and prayed for wisdom, power, and strength to fight the wolves. He knew that to survive, he must be strong not only physically, but also mentally and emotionally.

He pushed the remaining dogs out of the way and knelt as he looked upward. He raised his arms toward the heavens and said out loud, "I am a Cree warrior, and I will not be defeated easily. I will fight with all my will and strength until I die!" He beat his fist against his chest.

He could do nothing until sunrise, when the visibility would be better. At least the scratching of the canvas and digging around the tepee had stopped. He was marginally more comfortable inside with two fewer dogs, but not by much. He was still terribly cold and shivering uncontrollably. And he was desperately tired but found himself still unable to sleep as dawn came.

It had stopped snowing and was less cold. Isha had to dig himself out since the tepee was half covered with snow that obstructed the entrance. As he crawled out of the shelter and stood, he noted that the sled had been tipped on its side. He inspected it more closely and found that all the food and animal pelts were gone. The caribou meat, the pemmican, and the frozen fish for the dogs as well as all his other food supplies had been taken by the wolves. The tools and cooking utensils were scattered over the campsite.

This had been a well-thought-out guerrilla attack. Eliminating the food supply greatly diminished his and the dogs' strength and ability to continue to fight effectively. It became clear to Isha that the digging around the shelter by the wolves had been a diversionary tactic while the main group attacked and destroyed the sled and its contents. It had the added benefits of creating fear and lack of sleep for the man and enabling the wolves to eliminate two of his "slave dogs."

Isha was a disciplined hunter, and he would not let this setback affect his attitude. He was about two travel days from his village and safety. He was determined to make it. On the bright side, with very little cargo left to carry, the sled would be much lighter for the remaining dogs to pull.

Looking around the camp area, he noted several large tears in the canvas covering the shelter where the wolves had ripped it with their razor-sharp teeth and claws.

Isha craved sleep. He wanted to close his eyes, lie down, and drift off, but he knew he had to keep going to stay alive. With such extreme fatigue, he had to concentrate on each small task to avoid his mind wandering and drifting into a dream. He needed his mind sharp to fight the wolves or he could easily make a fatal mistake. When he noticed his mind drifting, he would shake his head and place some snow on his face. It took great effort to keep his mind alert, but he was determined to do it.

On the snowy ground close to the sled, he saw a blood trail leading down to the frozen lake. He followed the blood, hoping to find a dead wolf that he may have hit with a lucky shot. But as he reached the embankment of the lake, he saw the remains of the two dogs, Tipiskaw and Poslite. They had been torn to pieces and eaten. With the two dogs gone and all the food taken from the sled, Isha realized the wolf pack was now well fed. Since he saw no evidence of the wolves, they were probably sleeping now, but he thought, *I'll bet they have a sentry close by, ready to awaken the pack when I leave the camp.*

Isha had not slept in nearly seventy-two hours and was fatigued to the point of having delusional thoughts. He heard footsteps behind him, but when he turned around there was nothing. He began seeing movement in his peripheral vision, but when he turned and focused his attention, there was nothing. He realized that his fatigued mind was playing tricks on him and combatted it with mental discipline. He was hungry and had no food, which added to his problems.

He knew he had a long and dangerous day ahead of him. Besides Atu, the other remaining dogs, Sohkekan and Ashiny, were his two biggest and strongest dogs who pulled closest to the sled. He was glad these two remained because what he needed now from the dogs was strength and endurance. He didn't need them to be intelligent or fast—Atu would take care of that.

Unfortunately, he wasn't going to be able to feed the dogs. Isha then had a thought. He went down to the lake and picked up the scraps of skin, pieces of bone, and tissue that were left of the two unfortunate dogs. A hungry wolf pack doesn't leave much after they make a kill, but it was at least something to give a little energy to the remaining sled dogs. The hungry dogs relished the meager snack, unaware that they were eating their friends. He missed his two reliable dogs Tipiskaw and Poslite, but he didn't have time to grieve. He knew he and the remaining dogs were in grave danger. There was nowhere they could feel safe until he arrived at the village on Lake Kashapon.

Isha wanted something to bolster his spirits and prepare him for the anticipated terrible day ahead. He gathered some wood and made a small fire so that he could warm himself enough to stop shivering. He put some snow in a pot, and it quickly melted over the fire. He had some remaining coffee and threw a handful of grounds into the boiling water. The coffee tasted good and seemed to improve his spirits. After he finished the last cup, he put some of the coffee grounds into his mouth along with a large wad of tobacco. This gave him a little stimulation to fight off the pervasive and ever-increasing fatigue. It also temporarily suppressed his hunger.

He placed his rifle on top of the remaining cargo and placed his exceptionally large hunting knife at his waist outside his coat for easy access. "OK, now I'm ready to have at it. Let's go!" He gathered the three dogs close to him and hugged them in a bunch. He rubbed their heads and bellies and said, "Alright boys, I'm depending on you to get us all home. It'll probably take two more days and one more overnight." Isha harnessed the dogs, mounted the sled, said, "Let's go boys," and yelled, "MUSH!"

The sled went smoothly onto the frozen lake. Isha looked around and saw nothing but the frozen expanse of lake and wilderness. All was deathly silent. It was a sunny but cold day, a dramatic change in the weather from the day before. He thought, *At least I'll have one less thing trying to kill me.* The three remaining dogs were pulling strongly but with some extra effort. The heavy snowfall overnight made the sled more difficult to pull. It was the hardest on Atu since he was the solo lead dog running through the deepest snow. He made it a little easier for the other two dogs since they were following his path.

Isha realized that this was where the extra training could now be lifesaving for him and the dogs. Three dogs normally would be unable to pull a man and sled through deep snow. However, they were doing well. As Angus had said, what now seemed like years ago, this dog team was like no other. Isha knew the added snow gave a big advantage to the wolves, who were well adapted to running long distances in deep snow. Their legs were much longer than those of dogs, with large paws that acted like snowshoes. Hunting in these conditions was routine for them.

After an hour he looked to his left. There they were, loping along effortlessly just out of rifle range. He then looked behind him: more wolves, and yes, just out of rifle range.

Isha yelled at the wolves, "Well, did you sleep in today? Did you get a good rest?"

The wolves glared at him, silently keeping their distance. Isha tried to imagine what they were planning. He knew the giant wolf was up to something. The wolves traveled at a safe distance with Isha the entire day, loping steadily along, silently biding their time. Isha fleetingly thought that he could probably pick off the wolves at this long distance if he had a British Enfield rifle. However, the wolves would likely adjust and follow at a much greater distance after one or two were shot.

Isha began to think about how amazingly smart this giant wolf was. His strategies and methods of attack were well planned and executed. This wolf was like no other animal he had ever encountered. It seemed more human than animal, but how could this be? He had believed that animals didn't have the ability of future planning but only reacted to their immediate needs. He then thought of the Cree legend that Tiskigapon had told him regarding the evil monster from hell that hunted and killed human beings, the Wendigo. Could this be the present-day version of the Wendigo? According to the legend this was the same territory where the Wendigo lived. So many things Tiskigapon had told him had come true. Was he being chased and hunted by a monster? Monster or not, Isha would have to deal with it.

Isha continued to travel all day, followed persistently by the wolves. The dogs were holding up remarkably well. In approximately two more hours he would reach the end of the lake in the early evening. This was the beginning of his standard trapline trail, which was twenty miles from his village. This narrow trail was surrounded by dense forests and brush. He wasn't sure whether this was advantageous for him or the wolves. He began talking out loud to keep alert and awake: "I guess I'll find out. At least the snow won't be as deep on the narrow trail, and the snow underneath the recent snow will be packed. This will make it easier for the dogs to pull the sled. If we can get safely on that trail, we'll have a fighting chance to make it home alive. There's a shelter there as well. If I'm lucky, I could get some sleep there tonight, but I'm not going to count on it."

It was near dusk when Isha finally saw his shelter in the distance at the end of the lake. He looked around. No wolves were in sight, and he heard no howling. They had been following him all day, and now they were gone. He wondered where were. What were they planning now? He had a fleeting feeling of elation: *Are they gone? Did they come to the end of their territory and give up?* He placed his rifle in front of him, ready to grab it at a moment's notice. He took his mittens off so he could have the rifle in action quickly.

Close to the shelter was a mild incline up the bank from the lake. He recognized the large boulder and the adjacent small ravine that he considered the gateway to the Seal River country, the same place where he had stood many times since he was a boy and gazed upon the mysterious country beyond. On one side of the ravine was the five-foot cliff where the boulder was. The ravine made a clear passageway to the trail leading to Lake Kashapon. For the dogs to get up the embankment would require a short burst of speed. Then they could go on to the shelter, where they could camp for the night. He looked around and still saw no wolves. All was eerily silent.

He would finally be departing from this vast and terrible country, leaving the dreaded giant wolf and his bloodthirsty pack behind. He felt a glimmer of hope as evening approached and he came closer to the shelter.

Isha yelled his command to speed up: "MUSH, MUSH!" The sled easily came off the lake and into the small ravine. Within seconds Atu was at the top of the embankment at the edge of the forest, but then he stopped suddenly. Isha was thrown abruptly forward, catching himself on the wooden crossbar of the sled. Atu was aghast and taken completely off guard at the sight directly in front of him.

171

Atu was facing a large group of angry, snarling wolves. Baring their fangs and bristling their fur, they couldn't wait to pounce on their astonished prey. Mohegan and the pack had sprung the trap. They now had their prey where they wanted them after days of continuous stalking and wearing down Isha and the dogs. They were ready for vengeance for their beloved Sinapu and their other comrades who had been murdered by this hated man and his slave dogs. Now would be the finale of the contest of life and death.

Without hesitation Atu flung himself into battle with the wolves. He was fighting at least five wolves at a time. He was at a great disadvantage, as he was strapped into the harness, unable to maneuver while the wolves could dart in and out rapidly to deliver cutting gashes at will. One wolf grabbed his ear and tore it off. Another wolf grabbed his face and snout and began violently jerking his head, ripping Atu's face to shreds and extracting one eye. Another wolf bit Atu's body and ripped off a large portion of his muscular chest wall.

Opposite the small escarpment, the remainder of the pack had been quietly hiding in the bush. As soon as their comrades attacked Atu, the mass of wolves to the side of the sled shot out explosively toward Sohkekan and Ashiny. The dogs were taken by surprise since their attention was fixed on Atu and his fight. The mass of wolves hit the two unsuspecting dogs like a tidal wave. The two dogs were knocked into the air by the brute force of the onslaught of wolves crashing into them. Their leather harnesses pulled the sled upside down, flipping the dogs to the opposite side of the overturned sled. The dogs were trapped in their harnesses. They had very little ability to move or defend themselves while being slashed to pieces by the multitude of experienced killers.

The wolves had known Isha had to follow this path and knew exactly where to locate a good ambush. Like the excellent pack leader he was, Mohegan knew the topography of his territory well. This ambush site at the end of the lake marked the boundary line of the wolf pack's territory. Isha thought fleetingly, *I should've known this spot was dangerous for an attack*. The effects of his fatigue were showing. In a normal state of mind, he might have recalled this spot and somehow avoided it or taken another option and flanked the wolves, taking the offensive if that were even possible. He now had the dread feeling of a caribou trapped on all sides by deadly hunters.

Isha made a frantic grab for his rifle and put it to his shoulder, aiming at the nearest wolf. Suddenly, out of the corner of his left eye, he glimpsed the giant wolf leaping from atop the small cliff adjacent to where Isha was standing. Mohegan had been hiding from sight behind the large boulder. The giant wolf was already flying through the air with his mouth wide open, showing his huge fangs and ready to sink them into Isha's vulnerable neck and rip it away.

With lightning reflexes, Isha instantaneously ducked before he was hit by the giant wolf. Because of the quick reaction, Mohegan missed his neck but was able to sink his fangs deep into Isha's left shoulder and upper arm, ripping the muscle and tendons to shreds. At the same instant Mohegan delivered a bone-jarring body blow to Isha's 150-pound frame like a wrecking ball to a fragile building, knocking him off his feet and leaving him sprawling on the ground, gasping for air. The rifle was jolted out of his hands as his traumatized body was thrust into the snow, knocking his hat off. He was disoriented for a moment, not knowing what had happened. The world blurred into a mixture of agony and fear. His entire body felt fractured, like a piece of pottery hitting a concrete floor. He tried desperately to move but couldn't, knowing that at any moment he would be pounced upon and torn apart.

The razor-sharp fangs and powerful bite had easily penetrated Isha's coat and wool shirt like a knife through butter, leaving it in sheds. A huge gash in the tissues of his shoulder and arm was now exposed to the air, causing excruciating burning pain. Isha's immediate physical reflex was to yell, but the air had been knocked out of his lungs. He was eventually able to lift his head up out of the snow. He knew he had to recover quickly. Despite being severely wounded and traumatized, he raised his body to all fours. His vision was blurred because of the cold snow in his eyes. Isha's first thought was his rifle, which was now lying half buried in the snow close to the giant wolf. The wolf was just getting up after his great leap at Isha. Mohegan glared at Isha, baring his teeth with a furrowed nose and bristling fur. Mohegan growled in a deep, guttural tone as he stared into Isha's stunned eyes. The wolf thought, *Now I have you! You can do nothing without your magic stick. You are now a wounded weakling. I'm going to enjoy ripping you apart!*

Isha knew he wouldn't be able to get his gun before Mohegan could pounce on him. He thought, *Why doesn't the giant wolf attack me while he has the chance, now that I'm vulnerable?*

Despite his bleeding open wound and having had the wind knocked out of him, Isha sprang to his feet in the trampled, bloody snow. Out of the corner of his eye he noted another wolf, Wachak, flying at him from the top of the embankment where he had initially been attacked by the giant wolf. In a split second Isha grabbed his large hunting knife with his functional right hand, turned his body away from the wolf flying at him, and buried the knife to the handle in Wachak's chest in midair, puncturing one of Wachak's lungs. The mortally wounded wolf fell to the ground, profusely bleeding in the snow, gasping for air.

Isha now knew why the giant wolf hadn't lunged at him while he'd been getting up. Mohegan knew Wachak was about to jump on his back, and they would finish him together while he was down on the ground. This was a standard wolf hunting tactic, one wolf diverting the prey's attention while another wolf attacked from the opposite direction. The same thing had happened with the dogs. The initial attack had been on Atu in the front, followed by the unexpected attack from the side toward the other two dogs behind Atu. This attack had been performed with perfect timing and efficiency.

Mohegan was not expecting the severe injury to Wachak. He had thought that once the man's magic stick was gone, the man would be helpless. Now Mohegan saw Wachak mortally wounded, lying on the ground near death. This further enraged Mohegan against the evil and hated man. Mohegan now realized that man had a different magic tool to kill that he hadn't known about, not as powerful as the magic stick but still deadly—a knife.

Isha turned to the giant wolf and came face-to-face with him. Isha was bent over like a wrestler ready to attack. His only functional arm held the large knife outstretched in front of him, pointing at the giant wolf. Isha's other arm dangled helplessly at his side, bleeding profusely. They glared at one another, with Isha waiting for the giant wolf's next move. Mohegan was smart enough not to attack unless he knew exactly what he was getting into. Plus, he had the remainder of the pack fighting the dogs, and he thought that battle would be finished in short order. Mohegan saw blood streaming down the man's arm, dripping on the snow in a large puddle. He knew it was just a matter of time before the wounded man went down in a final onslaught after the pack finished with the dogs.

For a moment Isha and Mohegan faced each other, glaring into each other's eyes in a silent standoff, both waiting for the other's next move. The seconds seemed like hours. Both waited for any signs of weakness. Isha concluded that if the giant wolf were going to attack, he would already have done so.

Isha abruptly turned and ran to the three remaining dogs amid the bloody, vicious fight with the wolves. The nearly forty-member wolf pack were all over the dogs. Wolves were on the dogs' backs, on both sides ripping at the dogs' torsos, and in front of them biting their faces. There were so many wolves that he could barely see the dogs. Isha waded into the moving, roiling mass of fur, blood, and fangs as if entering the worst nightmare that any human being could imagine—except it was reality.

Isha entered a state of primal savage ferocity to kill and survive. He lost all higher conscious thought. He was fighting on the same level as the wolves, relying on wild, mindless aggression to kill or be killed. Welling up inside him from a dark place he'd never known was a cry he didn't recognize or understand: the howl of an enraged beast. He stood, knife in hand, screaming beneath the rising moon and darkening sky. He had turned into the wolf.

Isha disregarded the severe injury to his arm and shoulder. His deep fatigue evaporated. The adrenaline surging through his body obliterated all other factors except the urge to attack and kill. The bodies of the wolves and dogs pounded against his legs, oblivious to the man among them, completely absorbed with the fight in front of them.

Isha raised his knife and brought it down with a force that could have been generated only by his instinct of self-preservation. The long blade stabbed the nearest wolf in the face, blinding it in one eye. The wounded and permanently damaged wolf yelped in pain and ran away. Isha quickly turned toward another wolf that was on one of the dogs' back. With another powerful thrust, using his back and good shoulder, he stabbed the wolf deep in the side of the abdomen up to the handle of the long blade. He twisted the blade to create the maximum damage. With a strong heave of his functional arm, Isha catapulted the wolf into the air off the dog.

The mortally injured wolf landed on the snow away from the melee and lay there yelping and bleeding. Isha swung his knife at the other wolves as if wielding a scythe to harvest wheat, slashing away indiscriminately at the wolves' bodies and causing bloody, painful confusion among the pack as he seriously injured many. One wolf jumped from behind on Isha's back, biting him in the head. This caused a deep laceration on his scalp and tore away the hood attached to his coat. Isha quickly pivoted and slashed the wolf, throwing it off onto the snow-covered ground.

All the while Isha let out a continuous loud and deep scream that echoed through the forest above the horrific sounds of the savage fight. The wolves understood all too well that this man was a force to be reckoned with. This made them retreat before Isha's fearsome attack. They were temporarily stunned and intimidated as they saw their comrades seriously wounded, lying in the snow bleeding. They immediately recognized the animal ferocity of the man, which demanded respect. As apex predators themselves, they were witnessing an alpha male of a different species challenging them at their own level and claiming temporary dominance over them. This was the law of the predator, and they knew it must be obeyed.

They realized that the man was still dangerous and needed to be given temporary leeway. The wolves backed away, snarling, baring their teeth, and growling. They also knew it was a matter of time before they would tear the man and his dogs to pieces. The wolf pack had seen things like this many times before with other injured animals that were not quite ready to be taken down. They knew time was on their side. One thing the wolves knew all too well was patience.

Isha noted that the dogs were a bloody mass of hanging tissue and areas of absent fur with exposed muscle. However, they were still standing. Atu's face was a testament to the savagery he had encountered. His face was unrecognizable in its mangled state, like a large mass of bloody hamburger. The sled had been knocked upside down during the melee, spilling its contents on the ground. The canvas tarp, the musk ox blanket, and all the cooking pots and pans were scattered amid the surrounding wolves. There was no way Isha would be able to retrieve the rifle, let alone the other items, without exposing himself and being killed. With a tremendous burst of remaining adrenaline, he used his back and functional right arm to flip the sled upright on its runners. The wolves stood glaring, waiting for any sign of weakness. He jumped on the sled and at the top of his voice screamed, "MUSH, MUSH, MUSH, MUSH, YA, YA!"

With a resurgence of strength and force of will, Atu, Sohkekan, and Ashiny surged forward with their own burst of adrenaline and pulled the sled out of the ravine and onto the trail. They pushed aside the vicious crowd of wolves and drove forward like a football fullback driving through a defensive line. All the while the dogs were being snapped at and bitten by the surrounding wolves. The dogs simply disregarded the pain and focused on their goal to get beyond their attackers, out of the ravine, and onto the trail toward home. Isha knew Atu's strength and single-minded discipline were giving the other two dogs the will to survive and pull the sled. The dogs passed the ultimate test of strength, discipline, and loyalty by following Isha's commands despite the pain of having been bitten and harassed by the enraged, bloodthirsty wolf pack. Atu's iron will chose to ignore the pain and fatigue to continue with his duty for his kind master, for whom he was willing to pay the ultimate price.

The dogs successfully pulled the sled and Isha out of the ambush and away from the crowd of wolves onto the trail. Atu had to turn his head to one side for adequate forward vision since one eye had been ripped out. Isha quickly looked back and saw the giant wolf loping calmly after him, followed by the rest of the pack. Isha knew this fight was not over—in fact, it had just begun.

The Chase

Being in familiar territory encouraged the dogs. They knew they were heading toward the village, where there would be safety and comfort. Isha looked at his severely damaged limp left arm and noticed that it was bleeding profusely, with blood flowing down his arm and onto the snow. He realized that unless the bleeding was curtailed in short order, he would die. Because of the pulsatile flow, he knew that an artery had been severed. He needed to do something quickly, but he knew he couldn't stop because the wolves were close behind. He felt liquid that he knew was blood flowing down his neck and back from the gash on his scalp. He disregarded this wound because he couldn't do anything about it.

He bent over the sled crossbar, leaning on it while he removed the long red plaid scarf that Angus had given him from around his neck. With his good right hand, he began wrapping it around his damaged left shoulder and arm. He used his right hand and teeth to make a knot around the gaping wound. He pulled it as tight as he could, giving several strong jerking pulls with his head. This caused a tourniquet effect, significantly slowing the bleeding. He thought, *That's the best I can manage; it'll have to do.*

Suddenly the sled was thrown forcefully into the air. Isha had no time to think; he simply reacted by immediately taking his hand off his makeshift tourniquet and grabbing the crossbar he was leaning on. When he came down, one leg was off the sled, dragging in the snow. He was off balance, and he began to fall off the sled. He was barely hanging on with one arm. The sled began tipping to one side. Isha knew this meant impending doom if it fell over. In a near panic, he struggled to pull himself back, hanging on for life. He finally reestablished his balance and stabilized the sled back on its two runners. He thought, *That was close!* He had hit a large fallen tree branch hidden by the recent snow. There was no way he could have avoided the bump. He thought, *I've got to keep my hand on the bar with a good grip and concentrate on driving the sled and not worry about my injured arm and the wolves behind me. Who knows what may lie ahead on the trail, covered with snow?*

The wolves were confident, seeing the amount of blood on the trail.

They had done this thousands of times before—following wounded prey until it finally dropped from blood loss and exhaustion. They were in no hurry and expending very little energy. They could go on for days like this. This was now a routine hunt for them. They were encouraged when they saw Isha and the sled temporarily struggle to remain balanced. These experienced predators could smell fear in their victims, which excited them even more.

Isha had initially planned to stay overnight at the last shelter, but that was now out of the question. The sun had set below the horizon, and it was dark. He had no choice but to keep pushing ahead despite the difficulty of running the sled over rough terrain in the dead of night. This was not like the easy sledding of an open frozen lake. It took much more concentration and strength to control the sled and required maneuvering around obstacles, going up and down small hills, making turns in the trail, and crossing small frozen streams.

Fortunately, the sky was clear of clouds and the moon was bright. The trail was familiar terrain that Isha had trapped for years. He knew every turn, valley, and hill by heart. That was an advantage that Mohegan and the wolf pack didn't have since they were entering unfamiliar territory. Isha hoped there weren't any more hidden obstacles or for that matter a large tree that may have blown down in the recent blizzard, completely obstructing the trail. Isha knew that riding on the trail in the darkness, even with a full moon, was dangerous even without a pack of wolves close behind.

The bleeding had dramatically slowed with the use of the red scarf as a tourniquet. Isha realized that Angus's gift may have been lifesaving, at least temporarily. The bleeding from his scalp was now down to a trickle, dripping to his waist. He knew this was the least of his wounds and would not be life-threatening, as the injuries to his left arm and shoulder could be. The temperature was around ten below zero Fahrenheit. The cold temperature may have slightly improved the excessive bleeding by constricting the veins and arteries. He began to feel weak and lightheaded from blood loss. It had also been days since he had slept or eaten.

Isha was partially slumped over the wooden crossbar of the sled, supporting the weight of his damaged body. His mangled left arm was dangling by his side. He was now experiencing pain since the adrenaline surge of the fight had slowly melted away. Every minor bump or movement of the sled brought searing pain to his torn arm and shoulder. It was as if he were being stabbed by a red-hot knife with each minor jostle or movement. He grimaced and gritted his teeth, knowing he had to avoid thinking about the pain so that he could adequately function. He took a deep breath and slowly exhaled, trying to focus on driving the sled. He kept talking to the dogs, having a one-sided conversation with them not only to encourage them but to keep his mind off his pain. Talking to the dogs also kept his mind from wandering due to his severe sleep deprivation, which was again becoming a problem as the adrenaline of the fight dissipated. "You can do it, boys! Keep pushing, Atu. Stay strong, Sohkekan. You're doing great, Ashiny! We can still get out of this. We're not far from home, boys!"

The village was twenty miles away. The nearby shore of Lake Kashapon was fifteen miles away. During the ambush Isha had lost his fur hat and mittens. His wolverine-hide hood had been ripped off his coat, leaving his bare head exposed. These items are essential for survival in the subarctic north. His hands and his ears were now numb, and even the uninjured right hand was barely functional with decreased feeling because of the cold. Isha was slowly becoming hypothermic without these essential coverings protecting his head and hands. He began shivering uncontrollably. He was desperately thirsty from blood loss but had no way of alleviating this. He had to keep going.

Despite his weakened condition, he continued to encourage the three dogs, calling them by name and praising them. He realized that the three dogs were the key to his survival. It was not only Isha who was losing blood but all three dogs as well. They all had deep gashes and lacerations on their bodies and legs that continued to slowly bleed. The open wounds with exposed bleeding muscle began causing increasing pain as they toiled forward. They wanted to lie down but knew they had to keep running, not only for their sake but also for their master's. Sohkekan and Ashiny looked to Atu and followed his iron will to run despite the pain.

Isha looked behind and saw that the trail was covered in blood. The wolves were thirty yards back, seeming strong, confident, and patient. He could see the determined, glaring yellow eyes of the giant wolf focused on him. The giant wolf was leading the pack along the narrow trail, fully confident of the man's imminent demise, since he thought he had all the time in the world.

Mohegan, however, didn't know what was ahead. He didn't know about a village now fifteen miles away. All he knew was that he had several dying victims just ahead who were wearing down, and again, he had plenty of time. He expected them to collapse soon from blood loss, and then the final kill would be easy and safe. He would not take any chances with the man again, as he didn't know whether the man had any more magic devices.

Mohegan thought, *Man can do tricky, unexpected things, so different from other animals, but he is an animal that can be killed, nonetheless.* Mohegan would play it safe with this always dangerous ultimate predator. He was perfectly willing to let the man die slowly of blood loss. He had already seen too much to take this man lightly.

Isha could tell that Sohkekan and Ashiny were weakening despite being the strongest of his dogs except Atu. They were starting to drag their feet and turn their heads to look at Isha as if asking for help. Their heads began to droop toward the snowy ground. The sled began to slow down. They were now ten miles from the village and five miles from the frozen Lake Kashapon. Until now the dogs had been running on fear and adrenaline, which was now running out.

Isha called to the dogs, "Come on, boys, you can do it. Just get me to the lake; just give me five more miles!" Isha could feel a slight increase in speed after he exhorted the dogs, although he knew it was temporary. He also knew that Sohkekan and Ashiny could drop any minute. However, they were still responding to his encouragement and following their leader, Atu, directly in front of them.

Isha felt that if he was lucky, they had five more miles left in them, which would get him to Lake Kashapon, but there were five more miles after that to the village. What he would do after that, he didn't know. It might as well be five hundred miles to be so close yet so far from home and safety. He remembered his dream from a year before of being ripped apart and killed by wolves. He thought, *Could this have been a premonition sent to me by the Great Spirit, showing me how I am to die?* He recalled seeing seven wolves following him during the tribal caribou hunt that had vanished from his sight when he was about to shoot them. He knew he had killed seven wolves within the past several days. He wondered, *Could they have been the spirits of the wolves I recently killed, only in a reversal of time?* He quickly put the thought out of his mind. He then remembered the dream he'd had the night before leaving his home in which he and the wolf were staring at each other, unafraid, with a type of respect. He also remembered in the dream Atu's head being a blood-red smudge, which now appeared to have come true. He preferred to believe the latter dream, since it implied that he would somehow survive this terrible ordeal of which part had already come true.

Isha came to a straight and open area of the trail. He looked back and saw the relentless pack. His and the giant wolf's eyes met once again. The giant wolf's yellow eyes remained determined and focused on his prey. Isha had a temporary sensation of dread and felt a burst of perspiration when he saw his tormentor's malignant, cold eyes. He knew he had to maintain control over his thoughts as much as his body, as both were equally important for survival.

Mohegan was totally confident, as were the rest of the pack. The pack dropped back to an easier pace approximately eighty yards behind the sled. This was standard procedure for them, slowly wearing down their prey.

The sled was slowing further. The dogs' feet now fell heavily on the trail, pounding their bodies and increasing their pain and fatigue. With each step they felt stabbing pain from the open, bleeding gashes on their legs and torsos. Their feet were dragging in the snow, making it even more difficult to run and pull the sled. They were toiling far above their capacity to endure. The only things keeping them going were the exhortations from Isha and following their alpha pack leader, Atu, by blind instinctive reflex.

Suddenly Isha saw moonlight reflecting on a large area of open snow through the trees. It was frozen Lake Kashapon, about seventy-five yards away. "MUSH, MUSH!" he yelled. The two dogs raised their heads and gave one last big pull, giving everything they had to raise their feet and make one last sprint to the edge of the lake. They lunged to the bank of the frozen lake and collapsed. They had given their all and now they were done from blood loss, stress, hunger, and fatigue. They couldn't run anymore. Isha stopped the sled, mustered as much energy as he could, and ran to the dogs. With his only workable hand, he gave Sohkekan and Ashiny each a quick pat on the head and cut them loose from their harnesses with his knife. The two dogs lay in the snow, bleeding and panting for air, resigned to their fate.

Isha hoped the giant wolf and the rest of the pack would be delayed in the chase while taking care of the two hopeless dogs left behind. Perhaps that would allow him enough time to cover five miles and reach the village and safety. He didn't count on the single-minded determination and hate of the giant wolf.

There was no time to waste. Isha jumped back on the sled and yelled to his sole remaining dog, "MUSH, MUSH, MUSH! Atu, I know you can do it; just give me five more miles!" Atu quickly looked back with some regret at leaving his two friends behind, but he knew he had to keep going for his and his master's survival. He started to pull the sled, but it barely moved. Isha gave a heavy push to start the sled from its stationary position. He finally got some momentum and headed onto frozen Lake Kashapon. The sled began to slowly move over the frozen lake.

It was just one dog pulling Isha and the sled. For one dog to accomplish this feat was extraordinary, but man and dog knew they had no choice. Isha could tell Atu was struggling but giving everything he had. Isha realized that Atu truly was one of a kind, performing a nearly impossible feat of strength, endurance, and willpower.

Mohegan and the pack of wolves came upon the two sled dogs left behind by the edge of the frozen lake. The pack surrounded the two exhausted and spent dogs. The wolves couldn't wait to finish the job since these dogs had fought and bloodied them several hours before. Their instinct to kill was at its highest level. In an instant the entire pack was on the two dogs, tearing and ripping into their flesh without resistance from the exhausted duo.

Mohegan looked around. He didn't see the man! This was not what he wanted! Mohegan didn't want the dogs; he wanted the man and revenge for Sinapu. Mohegan knew it was important to sustain the pack's loyalty and morale, especially since Wachak and some of their comrades had recently been killed and some seriously wounded. He would not deprive the pack in the midst of their victory, even though it was incomplete.

He felt confident that he could finish the job alone. After all, his prey was in the process of dying. He wouldn't be surprised if he found the still bleeding man and sole remaining dog already dead, lying in the snow just ahead, given the amount of blood on the ground. Mohegan was an expert in evaluating blood loss and the condition of wounded animals. The pack would eventually follow once they were finished with their kill. It shouldn't take long for nearly forty wolves to finish off two severely wounded and exhausted dogs.

He could track the man and his remaining wounded slave dog for hours or even days if need be.

As the pack finished off their two helpless victims, Mohegan looked out on the frozen lake and saw the sled in the distance in the bright moonlight. Mohegan thought he could easily track his prey if he waited for the pack to finish the dogs; however, he wanted to keep the man in sight and finish him quickly.

Mohegan bolted after the sled by himself. He didn't need the pack to finish the job, and he was going to enjoy retribution better alone. He sprinted at full speed to catch the sled. By the amount of blood in the snow, he knew the man was in real trouble. The final sprint to bring down wounded prey was something Mohegan excelled at. His long legs flew through the snow like a machine, churning up small clouds of powderlike snow. His huge, powerful body flew through the snow like a speeding freight train with a fierce, deadly intent. He had plenty of energy to complete his mission. His eyes were now fixed on his approaching victim. His blood was up with growing anticipation of sinking his killer teeth into the hated man. With each leaping stride he was gaining rapidly. He relished the thought of crushing the man's bones with his jaws and then ripping him to shreds. He even imagined how the man's screams would sound during the deadly process and how he would relish inflicting excruciating pain on this hated enemy. He began to salivate at the mere thought.

Just as he was focusing on his prey, he noticed lights in the not-too-far distance. Mohegan was briefly stunned. He was not expecting to see this. This meant more men—a pack of them. A village! The sight sickened him, grouped together in a pack like his own kind only to destroy trees, plants, animals, and anything else they encountered. He recognized humans' ability to assert mastery over matter. It filled him with even more hatred and a renewed determination to kill the man before he reached his human pack. He knew it would be too dangerous to go into the human realm. If the man got there before he could bring him down, his intended victim would be safe. Mohegan now had just a short time to make the kill. He was in unfamiliar territory without his usual hunting pack to assist. He knew it was up to him to achieve the vengeance he so desperately wanted.

With single-minded focus, he began the final approach for the kill and turned his sprint toward his wounded and bloody victim.

Isha saw the lights of the village come into view. He had a flicker of hope, which had been rapidly slipping away from him. He now thought he just might make it home alive. He was so weak that he was barely able to stand. He was slumped over, leaning on the sled crossbar with his chest. His hands and head were freezing. He continued to shiver uncontrollably, but now he had a glimmer of hope.

He yelled to Atu, "Do you see that, Atu? We're almost there! Maybe just a mile or two."

Isha was unaware that Mohegan was closing fast. Atu saw the lights in the distance and began to pick up speed, but not nearly as fast as Mohegan closing behind.

Isha was oblivious to the threat rapidly closing in on him. Mohegan quickly assessed his prey, as he had done thousands of times before. The man's vulnerable head and neck were down, bent over the sled and not visible. His arms were too far away to grab, and there was nothing to grab hold of on the back. This left the legs as the best option for attack. Grabbing the legs and pulling him off the sled should work well. Breaking his leg during the process would work even better.

In a final powerful sprint Mohegan leaped into the air with tremendous strength and athletic coordination. He had timed the jump perfectly with speed and accuracy. He was flying at his prey like an arrow, and better yet, his prey was totally unaware. He opened his gaping mouth and buried his fangs deep in the man's calf. Mohegan could feel his teeth glance off the bone. In sudden shock and terror Isha gave a bloodcurdling, visceral scream.

He was violently pulled off the sled onto the frozen lake, knocking the air out of his lungs and plunging his face deep into the freezing snow. He instantly pulled his head up and gasped for air. His body was being dragged away by the giant wolf. Before he was totally taken from the sled, Isha grabbed the wooden crossbar with his remaining functional hand and held on with as much strength as he had left in a last-ditch effort to save himself. He told himself, *I'm not going to let go!* even though his fingers were being pulled away by the strength of the giant wolf.

Isha felt excruciating pain in his calf. He screamed as loudly as he could, hoping someone in the village might hear. He had the unbearable sensation of his leg being ripped apart.

It now became a tug-of-war between Atu and Mohegan with Isha in between, still holding on to the crossbar with one hand. Isha had a fleeting thought of just letting go, finally being done with the pain and overwhelming fatigue, just letting his spirit go and rest forever.

He thought, *NO! NO! I will not die this way. I refuse to let my body be ripped to pieces so close to my home and to be found by my family and neighbors. NO! NO! I am a Cree warrior! I will not give up!*

Isha was determined not to let go of the sled because he knew that if he did, the giant wolf would be standing over him, alone in the snow with his imminent death. The sled slowed markedly because of the counterpull of the giant wolf against Atu. Isha was being pulled in two opposite directions. He felt the tendons and ligaments of his leg being stretched and slowly giving way. Isha again screamed in utter agony. He felt his fingers starting to slowly slip. Mohegan could feel the weakness of the man and how helpless he was.

Mohegan thought, *You are nothing without your magical devices. You're not even as strong as a helpless caribou calf.* Mohegan gave several hard, powerful jerks to Isha's leg while violently shaking his huge head from side to side to loosen the man's grip and tear him away from his sled and his slave dog pulling in the opposite direction. Isha's body was flung like a rag doll, and he barely held on with his fingers to the wooden crossbar. He knew he couldn't hold on much longer. With each violent jerk of the giant wolf's huge head, Isha felt horrible pain with the tearing of his tissues. He screamed again, the sound emanating from the deepest part of his body as a horrific visceral reflex. Blood flew off his leg like a brush soaked with red paint being flung around with force, spattering the surrounding snow with large red drops.

The giant wolf now tasted the blood of the man, which inspired a primal reflex to finish the kill with even more savagery. Hate and rage flooded Mohegan's primitive psyche as never before. As soon as he got the man away from the sled, he would make the hated man suffer! He would not kill him quickly with a swift bite to the neck, crushing the windpipe. NO! NO! Not this time! Mohegan now planned on slowly eating him while still alive, one part at a time. First he would break the man's legs with his crushing jaws to immobilize him. Then he would tear open his belly and pull out his visceral organs to bestow the maximum amount of suffering and horror for what the man had done to his beloved Sinapu and his good friend Wachak. He wanted VENGEANCE! in its most severe form.

Amid the jerking of his body by the giant wolf, Isha felt his soft tissues, ligaments, and tendons give way with an audible pop. He immediately felt the worst pain he had ever experienced. He again let out a loud, uncontrollable scream as a wounded-animal response to imminent death. The sled lurched forward. Mohegan still had a mouthful of Isha's leg muscle and soft tissues but no longer held Isha's leg itself.

Isha still held of the sled handle with his only workable numb hand.

His body was being dragged through the snow by his powerful sled dog, Atu. Isha's entire calf muscle had been torn from the back of his knee, dragging the large piece of muscle behind the rest of his leg like a large, bloody steak attached to his ankle and trailing through the snow. Isha looked back and saw the giant wolf spit out the remnant of his flesh and then return to the attack. Mohegan sprinted toward Isha and the sled. The piece of Isha's leg muscle dragging behind him gave Mohegan further excitement in chasing the moving meat behind the man. The taste of the man's blood sent a thrill through Mohegan and drove him to attack even more aggressively than before.

Mohegan yearned to roll his body on the bloody, eviscerated corpse of the man, painting his fur red with the man's blood as a symbol of his vengeance for the entire pack . He was so close to victory that he could taste it.

With Isha's last remaining strength, he pulled his body up to the sled with his numb hand, flexing his biceps and forearm muscles as hard as he could. It was the strength that he didn't have, the last ounce of adrenaline in its final surge through his body. He used his pure will to slowly pull his damaged and spent body inch by inch up to the sled, all the while being dragged and barely holding on. He placed his chin over the crossbar, with both feet still dragging in the snow. Then, one shoulder at a time, he drew himself up until he was bending at the waist over the crossbar.

Mohegan was still much faster than Atu pulling the sled with Isha. He rapidly caught up to Isha's bloody, mangled body hanging half off the sled. Mohegan was close behind, ready to make one last lunge at the man. He knew this was probably his last chance to pull the man off the sled and drag him away. With tremendous power, Mohegan sprang into the air, mouth wide open, ready to rip his hated prey from the sled and finally satisfy his thirst for vengeance.

Gravity took over as Isha completely expended his strength. He flipped into the carriage of the sled headfirst, like a limp dead body randomly thrown into a grave. Mohegan missed the man's foot by inches. Isha could hear the clack of the giant wolf's teeth as they shut like a steel trap just behind him. Mohegan fell headfirst into the snow. He made a rapid recovery, springing up and bolting after the sled. His new objective was to stop and kill the dog; then he could get to the helpless man in the sled.

Isha had no control of his movement. His body landed face up on his back, with his head resting on the back of the sled. All his energy was now gone, no matter how much willpower he could muster. There was nothing left. He could no longer steer or guide the sled. It would all be up to Atu. All Isha could do was utter encouragement and try to give orders to Atu in his fading, barely audible voice. His mouth was terribly dry and pasty, making it difficult to even open it, let alone move his tongue. Isha's speech was now a garbled, slurred whisper. He couldn't make a sentence, only partial soft words that he struggled to get out.

The bottom of the sled was now a large pool of blood. Isha felt himself slipping away. The pain was now minimal because of his dropping blood pressure. He was in shock from excessive blood loss. He wanted to just close his eyes and go to sleep. However, he fought drifting off for fear that he might not wake again. He now knew what death was like, and it was staring him in the face. He was determined to keep fighting for life, but he knew he didn't have long. A great fear overtook him.

Atu, Isha, and the sled were now just one hundred yards from the village. Atu drew on his last bit of strength and began to sprint as fast as his ebbing power would let him before he collapsed from exhaustion and blood loss. His large, muscular body flexed with each stride, and he powered his sturdy legs high above the snow to gain more pulling strength with each step, like a hurdler in a hundred-yard sprint. He knew his master was dying and the giant wolf was again closing fast behind him. However, through his one remaining blurred eye, he could see his master's cabin. Hope was just a short sprint away.

Atu's body was screaming to stop and collapse, but his mind refused to listen, whipping his nearly dead body into one last race before it collapsed. He thought, *One last sprint and then I can die!* Atu was making his last full effort, not because of fear or mindless obedience but because of love and deep loyalty to his kind master, Isha.

Mohegan rapidly gained on the sled until he was nearly in the village. He knew there would be many magic sticks and many more unknown killing devices there. Getting too close to the village would be a significant risk to his life. Like the shrewd and cautious tactician he was, he abruptly stopped and watched as the sled glided away. He felt defeated and incomplete. He realized that the man would likely die soon, but he would lose the satisfaction of devouring the hated man himself.

In Isha's delirious state, he could see his cabin by the shore of the frozen lake. Atu lunged for the shoreline only a few yards away. His large muscles rippling in their last surge, Atu pulled the sled up the embankment into the village. The sled hit a large bump coming off the lake and onto the land, lifting the sled and Isha suddenly up into the air and then coming down with a thud. Atu pulled the sled up to the front door of Isha's cabin and collapsed in a bloody, exhausted heap. He had given his all, and now nothing was left.

Partially conscious, Isha leaned his head over the sled and looked back toward the lake. There he saw Mohegan, brightly illuminated by the full moon, silhouetted against the reflective glow of the snow. Mohegan, standing thirty yards away from the village, glared at Isha, raised his large head toward the moonlit sky, and gave a loud, long, haunting howl of hate unlike anything Isha had ever heard. The sound seemed to tear into his heart, as if it had teeth. He wondered for a fleeting second if this giant wolf was indeed the Wendigo.

Mohegan's prey had gotten away, but he had exacted a terrible price, giving him some, although incomplete, satisfaction. Mohegan, glaring at Isha, seemed to be saying, *You were lucky this time. Do not ever enter my territory again!*

It came to Mohegan that without the strong and determined slave dog at the head of the dog team, he would have killed the man on several occasions. He gave a grudging respect to the dog because this dog was like no other. Mohegan thought if the dog ever left the slavery of man and returned to the wilderness, Mohegan would gladly welcome him as a member of the pack.

Isha saw Mohegan turn and lope away into the dark distance as if returning to the darkness of hell from which he had come. Isha's body fell back, and he leaned his head against the back of the sled. He looked up at the moon and stars and thanked the Great Spirit for his deliverance. Isha tried to yell, but he didn't have the strength to utter a sound. He began to shut his eyes when he heard Atu bark frantically. Isha muttered softly, "IT'S OVER!" Little did he know that his struggle for survival was just beginning a new phase.

Isha couldn't move; he was barely alive. Atu lay in a patch of bloody snow, utterly exhausted, unable to move one more inch. Atu had some satisfaction in knowing that he and his master were safe from the jaws of the giant wolf. However, now they were facing another danger of slowly dying from their injuries. Atu realized that both he and his master needed help quickly. They could do nothing more to help themselves. The only thing Atu could do to save his master now was bark as loudly as he could to awaken the village for help.

Atu kept barking continuously, interspersed with a horrible blood-curdling yelping screech, a sound he had never uttered before but that anyone who heard it, man or animal, would know was a cry for urgent help from an animal in terrible distress. Instinct told him to keep barking and yelping until other men arrived. Atu barely had the strength to make a sound. He wanted to just lie down and sleep, but he again refused to allow his body that luxury. He needed to keep making as much noise as he could muster for his beloved master and friend.

The continued barking and yelping aroused many of the other dogs in the village until barking dogs were heard everywhere in the vicinity in response. The other dogs seemed to sense the extreme urgency of the calls from a dying animal. In their primitive way they were all telling men to wake up and help one of their own, now!

The Recovery

Cici finally came out of the cabin, bundled in a fur blanket. Some of the other villagers were emerging from their dwellings as well. Cici walked to the sled with her husband lying in the bottom, pale and unresponsive. Her eyes and mouth opened wide, and she let out a quick low scream. Cici yelled for help with a volume that she hadn't known she was capable of. She sat by Isha's side and held his head with her hands. She looked down into the sled and saw her husband lying in a large pool of dark blood. Several other villagers came running to their aid. Men picked up Isha's limp body and carried him into the cabin to his bed. In his delirious state, he felt a rush of warm, soothing air, a warmth he hadn't experienced in weeks.

Aingan was one of the first villagers to show up. Even tough Uncle Aingan was appalled at the sight of Isha's wounds. He applied continuous pressure to the main source of bleeding in Isha's leg. Cici tried to give Isha hot tea to warm his hypothermic body, but he was unable to take in the warming fluid.

Angus McDonald was awakened and summoned to Isha's cabin. He jumped out of bed, still in his sleeping attire, slipped his heavy coat and boots on, and jogged through the village to Isha's cabin, accompanied by one of the villagers. Angus was shocked at what he saw. His initial impression was that his good friend Isha was dead. He knelt beside Isha and placed two fingers on his neck to check for his pulse. It was still present but was weak and rapid. Angus told Cici to boil some water. He lit a kerosene lantern to improve the lighting in the dimly lit cabin. At Angus's direction, Aingan and Cici removed Isha's clothes to determine the extent of his injuries.

Isha's clothes were in tatters and soaked in blood, much of it frozen hard to the buckskin in congealed clots. Aingan stepped aside to let Angus work. Angus gently removed the blood-soaked red scarf from Isha's damaged left arm and shoulder.

Angus said, "Well, this scarf seemed to have come in handy." He thought correctly that the scarf had probably saved Isha's life, at least for the time being.

Angus had to suppress his emotions so that he could help his young friend in this critical situation. Isha's right leg was mangled. His calf muscle was severed at the back of the knee, hanging loosely away from his body. His Achilles tendon was partially severed, exposing his ankle and tibia bones. Angus's initial impression was that if Isha didn't die during the night, which was likely, he would eventually need his leg amputated to survive. Even the smallest amount of gangrene, if not removed quickly, would result in death in this preantibiotic era.

A deep gash in Isha's left shoulder exposed the shoulder joint and upper arm bone. Multiple tendons had been severed, but the main artery was fortunately intact. Most of the active bleeding had now stopped with continuous pressure. Angus also noted a deep laceration on the back of Isha's head. His hair was matted down with partially frozen blood. On further inspection Angus could see the white exposed skull at the base of the wound. However, there was no active bleeding.

Isha had a light purple discoloration to his nose, ears, and cheeks as well as his fingertips, consistent with frostbite. Only time would tell whether he would eventually lose these appendages. However, this damage didn't matter at present since it was not immediately life-threatening.

There was still one area of pulsating arterial bleeding in Isha's damaged leg. Angus applied pressure to the damaged artery and told Cici to get her sewing needle and thread. Cici ran across the cabin and began fumbling through her leather storage bags. She grabbed something and raised it up, saying, "I've got it!"

She ran to Angus, who took it with his right hand as he kept pressure on the bleeding artery with his left. Now, with all of his clothes removed, Isha began to shiver uncontrollably. The shivering was so extreme that it affected his entire body like a seizure. Cici was directed by Angus to bring hot towels from the boiling water and place them over Isha's hypothermic body. This reduced the shivering while Angus held direct pressure on the actively bleeding artery in the leg. Angus told Aingan to hold the leg still. Cici placed her head next to Isha's to give him emotional support even though he was unaware. She made the sign of the cross on his forehead with her finger and then kissed his cheek.

With careful and steady movements, Angus sutured the artery and skillfully tied it, completely stopping the blood loss. He then sutured the slow, oozing veins in Isha's shoulder and closed his scalp wound. Angus cleaned and washed the wounds with saltwater. This is usually quite painful, but Isha was oblivious in his current state. Angus placed the calf muscle back in the deep open gash in Isha's leg. He thought the muscle would eventually die and turn gangrenous, but for now it was worth a chance to save it. The muscle would at least temporarily cover the exposed blood vessels and bone to avoid the detrimental effects of desiccation from the open air. He tightly wrapped all the wounds in cloth. This was all he could do for now. Angus and Cici washed and cleaned Isha's body and placed thick fur blankets over him. Angus didn't think Isha would make it through the night, but he didn't say so to Cici.

Angus told Cici he would return in the morning to check on Isha.

Isha was extremely pale, with an ashen gray color. He was barely alive, more like a corpse than a living human being. Aingan had seen many injuries in his lifetime and was almost certain that Isha would die during the night. He wanted to be with Cici when this happened. While Cici sat at Isha's side, Aingan sat solemnly in a corner of the cabin, totally silent, waiting for the inevitable.

When the villagers looked into the sled and saw the amount of blood, they couldn't imagine how Isha was still alive. They didn't realize how much additional blood had been lost along the trail for the past twenty miles. People who had lost as much blood as Isha usually died within twenty-four hours. If they did survive initially, they frequently died weeks to months later because of their weekend condition.

Isha opened his eyes and looked up at the sky, which was a brilliant blue. He couldn't remember the sky ever being such a vibrant color. He was on an island, standing on a sandy beach looking out at a beautiful lake that seemed vaguely familiar. Several green Islands, like floating emeralds, seemed to glisten in the distance. The bright sun shone on the lake, creating reflections like sparkling diamonds and shooting rays of golden sunlight. He was warm and without pain. There was a calm in his spirit and a strange sensation of fulfillment and happiness. He noted that his injuries had completely healed. His bare feet felt good on the warm sand with the cool lake water gently washing over them. He began to wonder where he was, so he walked down the beach. He suddenly recognized this island as the place where he and Cici had been several times before their marriage and shared many fond memories. Yet the island was somehow different. It was more vibrant, almost glowing. An otherworldly quality of this place made it seem as if the ground itself were alive. He felt a sense of awe and wonder. His eyes were wide open with amazement, and his mind was racing with questions.

As he walked farther down the beach, he saw some people in the distance, sitting by the lake around a campfire. He wondered if they could tell him where he was. As he approached the two men and one woman, he noted that there was something familiar about them. They were all young, in their mid- to late twenties, in the prime of their lives. He could smell the wonderful aroma of cooking food. He noticed that they had coffee brewing as well.

As Isha drew close to the trio, one of the men stood up, smiled, gave Isha a big hug, and said, "Have a seat, Isha. We've been expecting you, but not quite so soon. Your grandfather, Sechawee, and I caught quite a few lake trout today and decided to have a shore lunch. We were having so much fun catching them, we threw most of them back. A few were big ones too. It was quite a day."

It suddenly came to Isha: *It's my father, only very much younger than I remember. Yes, I remember the voice of my grandfather in the other man and his characteristic smile and mannerisms. But now he's a young man! How can this be?*

"Dad?" Isha said in astonishment.

"Hello, son, sit down and have some lunch." Isha sat down with the others on the warm, comfortable sand gently sloping toward the beach. "Meet your sister, Sechawee." The young woman gave Isha a big smile. She was beautiful and had a family resemblance. Isha knew he'd had an older sister who had died in infancy. Sechawee got up and placed some fried trout, potatoes, and onions on a plate and handed it to Isha along with a cup of coffee. "Nice to meet you, Isha. Your wife is a wonderful lady." Isha wondered how Sechawee knew his wife, but he wasn't going to ask. So many questions hung heavy in the air.

Isha couldn't remember ever having such a delicious meal. The coffee was the best he had ever tasted—hot and strong, just the way he liked it, only much better.

"Besides the trout, which is great, what are the other things I'm eating? I've never had anything like this. It's wonderful, and what are those little black spots on the food?"

"Oh, we thought you'd like it. They're fried potatoes and onions. The little black spots are pepper."

"I've had wild rice and arrow-plant root, but nothing like this. Besides it being delicious, it's got a bit of kick," Isha said.

The other three laughed. "That kick you talk about is the pepper," Sechawee said.

Isha wasn't going to ask what pepper, potatoes, and onions were. He had too many other important questions.

As they all sat on the beach, eating and looking out on the beautiful lake, Isha said, "Am I dead? Is this heaven?"

The others chuckled and looked away without answering.

"Does the Wendigo live around here?"

They seemed alarmed at the question and said, "Oh my, no! We wouldn't want it around here."

After finishing lunch and downing several cups of coffee, Isha heard a distant subtle sound from the beach where he had just been. He listened intently. It was a soft voice saying his name. He looked in that direction but saw nothing. Isha looked back at the trio.

His father said, "You'd better see who's calling you, Isha." Isha again looked down the beach and saw nothing. he was confused. The voice kept calling his name, now a bit more loudly. He looked back at the others, wondering what this voice was, but they had vanished along with the cooking utensils and fire.

He stood up and yelled, "Dad, Grandfather, Sechawee!" He didn't want them to leave. He missed them already. He wanted to talk with them about so many things. Isha didn't want to leave this wonderful place, but he decided to take his father's advice and investigate the voice that was calling him. He began walking down the beach toward the voice in the direction from which he had come.

Isha opened his eyes and saw the Cici looking at him, calling his name. He immediately felt terrible throbbing pain in his wounded leg and arm. Cici seemed overjoyed that Isha had opened his eyes and hugged him, saying, "Isha, you're alive! You've been unconscious all night."

Aingan jumped up from his seat in the corner of the cabin when he saw his nephew's eyes open. He knelt by his side and asked, "What happened?" Isha said only two words, "GIANT WOLF." He took several cups of hot Labrador tea. Aingan was amazed that Isha had made it through the night. However, he knew there was a long road ahead and not to get his hopes up too high.

Later that morning Angus came in and, like Aingan, was amazed and relieved that Isha had made it through the night. Angus carefully removed the dressings and looked at Isha's wounds. The tissues appeared healthy with adequate blood supply, including the calf muscle, which he thought to be a near miracle. However, Angus knew they had made it only over the first hurdle of surviving the initial trauma. The next hurdle was after a week, when tissues would either live or die and when the ever-present risk of gangrene and infection would become obvious. If the calf muscle appeared to be nonviable or if there was evidence of gangrene, the leg would need to be amputated. However, Angus didn't think Isha could survive the operation, especially in this primitive location.

As the days passed, Isha had to be slowly hand fed as frequently as he could tolerate. He was given bone-marrow broth until he was able to tolerate solid food. The pregnant Cici and her mother cared for Isha and the three-year-old child. Aingan supported them by bringing food and other materials.

Angus checked on Isha twice daily and began to be guardedly optimistic. Fourteen days after Isha's injuries, Angus checked the wounds. The tissues continued to be healthy with no signs of infection or gangrene. He was amazed. However, unless something was done soon to repair the severed tendons, Isha would never walk again or have the use of his left arm. The severed tendons had retracted. After fourteen days they would scar and be unable to be repaired. Angus knew Isha needed extensive surgery; however, it would take weeks of travel over 650 miles of rugged bush in winter to get to the nearest modern hospital. He knew he had to do the best he could with the primitive surgery he knew.

Angus realized that the procedure would be terribly painful and brutal. Adequate anesthesia was unavailable, as were sterile surroundings and proper surgical instruments. There was a good chance that Isha would not survive the operation because of the stress alone, let alone the other factors. Isha was unable to get out of bed and could barely raise his head. However, his condition had vastly improved since his initial injury.

Angus sat at Isha's bedside and explained the situation. Isha said,

"I would rather die than be unable to walk and provide for my family. I refuse to be taken care of like a baby. I refuse to be a burden! Do what you can, Angus. I know you will do your best. If I die, it is the will of the Great Spirit. Death would be better than being an invalid. I am a Cree warrior!"

"Yes, you are. You are truly a brave Cree warrior, my friend."

Isha attempted to sit up but immediately felt lightheaded and dizzy. His skin became even more pale than it already was. He fell back down in bed, exhausted from the most minor movement. Upon seeing this, Angus knew that Isha was terribly anemic from blood loss. He began to have great concerns about Isha's ability to make it through any kind of surgery.

Angus knew Isha desperately needed a blood transfusion, but again, under the circumstances this was impossible. He realized that if there was any blood loss at all during the procedure, Isha would die. Angus also knew that performing surgery on inflamed and swollen tissues fourteen days after the initial trauma would cause excessive bleeding with the slightest manipulation. Angus had great trepidation about performing such a complex operation that he had never done before. All he knew was that tendons and ligaments performed like ropes and pulleys to a living muscular machine, and these structures needed to be repaired if Isha was going to retain the use of his arm and leg.

Angus knew he had to reattach the tendons to the bone. This would entail suturing the tendons to the outside of the bone, which is one of the most sensitive and painful parts of the body. He knew if the operation was unsuccessful, Isha would need an amputation, which he realized Isha could not survive. Isha fully understood the consequences, which were clearly laid out for him by Angus.

Cici knelt beside Isha and stroked his hair. She said, "I will be with you tomorrow. I will always be by your side."

"No, I will not allow you to see me suffer and possibly die! You must stay here with our son. I will see you soon enough after the operation, or I will see you later in paradise."

Angus was standing across the room and said, "It's best you stay here, Cici. It'll place more stress on Isha if you are there, and it would be quite difficult for you as well. I'll talk to you after we're done."

Cici lowered her head and began to cry. Isha softly grasped her hand and looked at his wife. "You must be strong. I will live. I have gone through too much to die now. Somehow, I feel the Great Spirit is with me. I WILL LIVE!" Cici again made the sign of the cross on his forehead with her finger and bowed her head in prayer.

Angus was not optimistic about his good friend's future. He thought Isha had a fifty-fifty chance of surviving the operation, but in the long run his chances of survival would be 5 percent at best. However, he didn't say this to the couple and presented an optimistic outlook to give them hope and confidence for the upcoming surgery. Angus knew from long experience that a positive attitude was essential for anyone who is critically ill. He had many times seen that when an injured person said they were going to die, they usually did. Angus thought Isha's will to survive was the most important thing in his favor.

The next day, fourteen days after his initial injury, Isha was taken by stretcher to the trading-post cabin and placed on two long wooden tables that had been moved end to end next to each other. A smaller table was placed adjacent to the other two as a workspace for instruments. Angus needed all the light he could get. Two lanterns were placed close to the tables, and all the shades on the windows were opened. A large fire was made in the fireplace with boiling water in a large pot.

Angus had a half-full bottle of laudanum, an opioid type of painkiller, which wouldn't be at all sufficient. He had used nearly all the pain reliever for a broken leg he'd set several months previously. He planned on a two-stage operation, with the leg today followed by the shoulder the next day to minimize the stress on Isha's fragile body. Along with the laudanum, Angus brought a bottle of his personal scotch whiskey that he kept hidden and used only on special personal occasions.

Angus had heard of the theory of unseeable "germs" causing infections, and he knew certain chemical agents and application of heat to instruments reduced infections. He washed his hands and poured whiskey over them. He gave Isha the bottle of scotch along with half the bottle of laudanum, with the remainder to be used for the next day's procedure. Isha swigged down several gulps of whiskey along with the laudanum. He grimaced after taking the whiskey and said, "How can anyone stand to drink this stuff?" Angus smiled as he looked down at Isha and said, "It's an acquired taste." Isha shook his head and lay back on the pillow.

Angus placed several crude instruments in boiling water and then placed them next to Isha on the worktable on a cloth that had been boiled and dried. On the table were long-necked pliers, scissors, tweezers, gauze, and a needle with silk thread. Isha was then held down by Aingan and several other men and given a thick wooden stick to bite on. Isha noticed that Aingan was looking away to avoid witnessing the surgery.

Remembering what Aingan had said to him long ago after having his face split open by the bull moose, Isha said, "What's the matter, uncle, are you afraid of a little blood?" Isha laughed and then put the wooden stick between his teeth and laid his head back. Aingan was silent and closed his eyes as he held his nephew's foot even tighter.

After dousing the wound and his hands with scotch whiskey, Angus gently grabbed the tendons of the calf muscle with the long-necked pliers and tweezers. The tendons had retracted deep into the surrounding tissue. Angus had to tease and dissect the tendons away from the inflamed and swollen anatomic structures. This necessary maneuver was tremendously painful. Isha arched his head back and bit into the wooden stick, leaving deep indentations in the wood. His breathing was rapid and heavy. He didn't make a sound except for his irregular breathing. Beads of sweat poured down his face. Angus took meticulous care in the dissection to avoid damaging any nerves or blood vessels. The more meticulous and careful the dissection, the longer the surgery would take. However, the longer the surgery, the more pain and stress would be inflicted on Isha's fragile body. Angus tried to operate with care yet move as quickly and safely as possible.

Isha could feel the most minor touch to his tissue with excruciating severity. After hours of intense surgery and utter agony for Isha, Angus was finally able to free the tendons from their retracted position and suture them to the severed ends on the outside of the bone at their insertion sites. He did this with a straight needle and silk thread used for embroidery beadwork. Isha hadn't realized that the pain could get any worse, but it did. It was just as bad as when the giant wolf had torn his leg apart.

Angus then repaired the partially severed Achilles tendon. At the termination of the procedure, he washed the open wound with saltwater and again doused the area with whiskey. He then wrapped the leg in gauze after applying freshly boiled caribou moss.

Isha didn't move an inch during the procedure, nor did he scream. The pain was excruciating, but he refused to be defeated by it. He looked upon the pain as a new adversary to be conquered. He knew numerous villagers were waiting outside the cabin for news of the surgery. He would not give in or show weakness. After all, he was a brave Cree warrior! A surge of pride in his nephew ran through Aingan, greater than ever before. He felt honored to be the uncle of such a brave young man.

At the end of the surgery Isha was so drenched in sweat that it appeared as if he had jumped in a lake. Aingan and the other men holding Isha down felt traumatized themselves after the surgery. Isha was taken back to his cabin and slept all day.

The surgery on the shoulder was performed the next day. The procedure went well and was not as extensive as the operation on the damaged leg the day before. Only time would tell whether either surgery was successful. Angus again was silently pessimistic.

After the surgery, the only pain medication Angus could offer was willow bark to chew, which is an age-old Native remedy for pain. The bark contains a chemical like aspirin. Isha refused any more of Angus's scotch whiskey.

Angus visited Isha's house to care for his wounds. He removed any unhealthy tissue carefully with scissors and a sharp knife. He cleaned the wounds twice daily with water sterilized by boiling. The process of dressing changes was painful. Isha dreaded them but knew they were important for his recovery. Isha was given a wooden stick to bite on, again with no anesthetics available. Angus applied the moist caribou moss against the wound and then wrapped dry cloth bandages over the moss. This, in today's medical care, is called a wet-to-dry dressing change and remains the mainstay of medical therapy for open infected wounds. Caribou moss has the effect of absorbing any drainage from open wounds and has an antibiotic effect. This had long been known among the Natives of the region.

The terrible experience had changed Isha. He grew past the pain of his body, past the fear of dying, past the concerns of conscience that kept a man small. He stood huge and full of icy determination to heal his body and heed what he had learned from the Great Spirit.

In time Isha began to sit up without becoming lightheaded. His appetite increased. After a month Isha's pale appearance improved. In two months he was able to carefully use his damaged left arm to some extent. His previously flaccid, unmovable left fingers began to move and grasp things. Angus was shocked one day to see Isha feeding himself with his injured hand. He'd made a remarkable recovery but still had a long way to go. Isha still had significant limitation of movement of his injured extremities even though his wounds were healing well. He was able to limp around the village with a crutch for balance, but he still became easily fatigued. Angus didn't think Isha's mobility would improve further without expert advanced care from the white world. Isha would not be able to provide for his family with his present disability. But at least he was alive with his extremities intact, even though they weren't functioning well. The areas where he'd been frostbitten healed with some minor scars.

Winnipeg

In the early spring, after the ice melted from the rivers and lakes, Isha made a long journey to Winnipeg, Manitoba, by canoe with his uncle Aingan. Angus gave Aingan and Isha a map and compass as well as descriptions of landmarks for the long journey. The two were not accustomed to using a map and compass since they knew their fishing and hunting grounds by heart from years of use. However, they both easily picked up the abstract concept. The journey would be particularly difficult for Isha since he was still weak and totally dependent on Aingan. However, Angus was more concerned about when they finally arrived in the big city and how they would adapt to a completely foreign and intimidating new environment. Angus knew culture shock could be more debilitating than anything the two men might have faced in the bush.

Angus described where to go and what to do when they reached Winnipeg, since he was familiar with the place. He drew a small map of the city with the locations of the hospital, boardinghouse, and other places that would benefit Isha and Aingan. However, he could tell they didn't comprehend the challenges they would face. Angus warned them that the city would be vastly different than what they were accustomed to and could be quite frightening. He told them not to fear.

Isha and Aingan thought it amusing. "Fear, ha! We fear nothing!" Isha said. "What could I possibly be afraid of after having survived being torn to pieces by a giant wolf?"

It was a long and arduous trip, nearly 650 miles over many rivers and lakes of remote wilderness. The journey took over six weeks. Isha was still too weak to walk over rough terrain for any distance, so Aingan carried Isha piggyback, like a pack filled with lightweight clothing, across portages and forest trails along with their canoe and camping equipment. It was fortunate that Aingan was so strong and dedicated to his nephew's well-being.

During his long trip, feelings of hate and anger at the giant wolf slowly began to creep into Isha's mind. He looked at his damaged extremities, which had once been strong and limber. From the pinnacle of his manhood, he was now reduced to a cripple being carried by his uncle. As the days went on, his anger increased as his self-esteem decreased. He was silent about his feelings, making them even more intense. He brooded about the wolf mainly at night, making it difficult to sleep. At times he would sit up, thinking his head was going to explode. He thought, *I would have been a wealthy man if I had brought back all the furs I had trapped. People would have admired what I had done. Angus and Cici would have been proud of me, as would my father.* He thought of the wolf as a demon, the Wendigo, that must be hunted down and killed. He began thinking of ways to wage war on this terrible beast and to regain the sacred region of his ancestors. This would require many other hunters from the tribe joining him in going to war, as had been done in the distant past against other tribes.

As the days progressed, his anger slowly simmered until thoughts of a future war with the wolf became all-consuming. He began to plan an expedition into the Seal River country with groups of hunters to set up multiple ambush sites with caribou carcasses as bait and an extensive trapline targeting wolves. However, the giant wolf might be intelligent and cunning enough to avoid this strategy. Isha had firsthand experience with this wolf and knew he was like no other. If the trapping and ambush plan didn't work, he thought of the use of poison. But this would mean indiscriminate killing not only of the wolves but of all meat-eating predators, leaving a large kill zone filled with dead animals. The fur could be harvested, but there would be nothing left to trap for years to come.

He even considered burning the entire region by forest fire. The dry period during the summer, when there was a predominant south wind, would be the perfect time for multiple large bonfires at different locations. The pine, spruce, and birch forests would burn easily because of the resin produced by the bark. There was a significant amount of deadwood in the forest as well. *Yes,* he thought, *burning the region would be good!* This would drive all animals away from this evil land, including the wolves, destroying their productive home and food supply. The sacred black rock would be impervious to the fire, sparing the only positive spot in the region. He thought of using all four methods at different times: trapping, ambush, poison, and then fire. He wanted the entire Seal River country annihilated. *After all,* he thought, *the giant wolf is just an animal—a clever one, but still an animal that can be killed. The earth would be better off without this monster along with the evil presence of the Seal River country.*

Upon reaching Winnipeg, Isha had to do all the talking since Aingan spoke only Cree. There Isha underwent several reconstructive surgeries. The money they had was not enough to pay for the entire hospital stay, but he was taken as a charity case by the hospital. For a while Aingan stayed in a boardinghouse not far from the hospital. Aingan was overwhelmed by the mechanized, fast-paced white world. He had never realized how many people there were in the world. He felt like a child in this hectic, noisy environment, filled with the strange, intimidating machines of 1914.

Other Indigenous men were staying in the boardinghouse, but none were Cree, and they didn't know his language. They had different mannerisms and different ways. Most of them had had far more contact with the white world than Aingan's tribe. Even they looked upon Aingan as some primitive beast. Most of these men wore part white and part Native clothing. Nearly all of them wore leather boots manufactured in the white world, as opposed to Aingan's buckskin mukluks. Aingan thought he would investigate buying some boots at Angus McDonald's trading post when he returned to the village since they appeared beneficial, especially over rocky terrain.

Aingan stayed in a large dormitory that contained over twenty beds. The Native men staying in the boardinghouse were there for only a few days at a time to bring furs to sell, obtain supplies, and then return to their villages. These other men weren't friendly, possibly because of Aingan's fearsome appearance or because of the language barrier. He became morose sitting in his boardinghouse surrounded by unfriendly strangers, staring at blank walls with nothing to occupy his mind. He felt caged. He missed sleeping in his comfortable cabin with his affectionate, plump little wife.

Aingan quickly found that he was easily cheated out of his money since he didn't know the language or the cost of food and other items. He often saw other people giving far less money to shop owners than he for the same item. Not knowing the language and simple mathematics was a huge barrier for him in this strange new world.

People in the city gave him long stares and frequently tried to stay as far from him as possible. Many moved to the other side of the street to avoid coming close to Aingan because of his huge, menacing appearance, long, matted greasy hair, and buckskin clothes. His pants and shirt were deeply stained with a mixture of dirt, grease, and old blood. His clothes had the appearance of never having been changed from the first day they'd been put on.

To avoid the unfriendly and claustrophobic conditions of the boardinghouse, he began taking long walks. Aingan became hungry walking aimlessly around the streets of Winnipeg and didn't have his supply of pemmican readily available. He walked into a diner and sat down at a table. It catered mainly to workmen and was nothing fancy. When a waiter came over, Aingan pointed to a plate of food being eaten by a man next to him since he couldn't read the menu. The waiter shook his finger at Aingan and pointed to the door. Aingan wasn't quite sure what he was being told and was hungry, so he stared silently at the waiter. The waiter seemed upset. Aingan again pointed at the plate of food next to him and took out a wad of paper money to show that he could pay for a meal. The manager of the diner came from the back and confronted Aingan. The manager made himself clear, raising his voice and pointing to the door. Aingan now understood and left the diner, placing the money back in his pocket. He wandered around the city, entering several diners and restaurants with the same outcome.

He was constantly yelled at to get out of the way of carriages, streetcars, and the newest thing, the first automobiles. It seemed to Aingan that the white world thought of him as an animal. This ostracism by the city dwellers began to slowly erode his sense of self-worth. He felt a loneliness he had never felt before in all his years of living by himself in the bush. When he returned to the boardinghouse, he felt just as alone as he did walking around the streets of Winnipeg. There was no place he could go to feel peace and comfort.

He now realized what Angus had been trying to tell him before he and Isha had left. He felt a different kind of fear. It was worse than an attack from an animal or a hostile tribe. This was a slow, pervasive form of decay, rotting his inner strength. Something unseen, like a disease stealing his soul. He felt as if a heavy, dark blanket had been placed over him, making him unable to see light or true reality.

It seemed that the Great Spirit was absent from this strange world. He concluded that this place was a realm of evil spirits. The city was busy and filled with people, yet in a way lifeless. The people in the city didn't seem human to Aingan.

He decided to leave the boardinghouse and make a camp several miles away from town on Lake Winnipeg. Here he fished and hunted for food to supplement his regular diet of pemmican. He could stay away from what he thought of as the scheming, confusing, unfriendly city. Aingan returned weekly for provisions and to see Isha. During Aingan's visits to the hospital, Isha could tell his uncle was not doing well in this strange environment. Aingan never admitted to this, however, and put on an outward show of bravado. Isha realized how similar he and Aingan were to wolves: lonely and not as effective without the socialization of their own pack. Both Isha and Aingan couldn't wait to return to their village, where they would feel like men again, in control of their lives and futures.

Isha was placed in a hospital ward of nearly forty men with varying types of illnesses and injuries. He received good care from the surgeons and nursing staff. Everyone was friendly and helpful. Upon viewing some of his fellow patients, he felt a comradery with some others with severe injuries. During his hospitalization he made friends with some of the other patients and left with a much greater command of the English language and respect for white culture. Nevertheless, he felt out of place and terribly lonely, just as Aingan did. He too felt that the city seemed devoid of the Great Spirit. He realized that without the Great Spirit's presence, one's soul and therefore one's strength would slowly erode.

One day in the hospital Isha was given a dinner of meatloaf along with fried potatoes and onions. "This is the food I ate when I was in heaven!" Isha said. He was overjoyed and began to excitedly tell other patients that this food was made in heaven.

His neighbor in the next bed said, "Yeah, it's good, but nothing out of this world."

Isha couldn't understand how his fellow patients could take eating such wonderful food so lightly. Isha asked if the orderly could bring him pepper. He poured the pepper over everything. Isha then realized that too much of a good thing can be bad. Nonetheless he relished the meal and asked for more. Isha now knew that it wasn't just a dream he'd experienced because he had never eaten that food before and recognized it immediately. He didn't even know what those food items were. He had left heaven before he could ask his relatives about potatoes, onions, and pepper or how they were grown. He wondered if being given this "heavenly" food had been planned by the Great Spirit to encourage him and lift his spirits in a time of need.

The surgeons in Winnipeg told Isha that without the earlier surgery performed by Angus, he would have lost his leg and the use of his left arm. The surgeons commended Angus for his good technique, surgical judgment, and excellent postoperative care, even though Angus had never been to medical school. He'd received his training from life experience in the bush out of necessity and because he had a large amount of common sense and courage. The doctors also told Isha that it had been a miracle that the wound hadn't become infected. The surgeons became interested in Angus's use of caribou moss as a treatment for traumatic open wounds.

During Isha's hospital stay he began having vivid dreams again nearly every night, but markedly different than before. They didn't involve him and were more complex. Each dream told a story of the giant wolf's life, including names and places. It was like hearing a story with a narrator, with him being totally detached. Every morning upon arising, he would shake his head and recount the dream so he wouldn't forget it. He wanted to remember so he could retell them to Angus and Tiskigapon. In Cree culture dreams are important and are thought to come from the Great Spirit. By now Isha knew from his experience not to take dreams lightly. These recent dreams weren't vague, abstract, or difficult to understand, as in the past. He wondered if the medications he was given had something to do with the dreams; nonetheless, he was taking them seriously and with great interest.

Each successive dream built upon the previous night's dream, creating a confluent narrative involving Mohegan and the others. The names of Wachak, Sinapu, Nagan, Talgu, the old moose, and Otho were like burning embers in his mind that couldn't be ignored or forgotten. These dreams affected Isha powerfully. Upon awakening, he felt as if he had visited another world, as if coming out of a trance, yet energetic with a clear mind. It seemed that the Great Spirit was forcing him with great power to pay close attention. He began looking forward to sleep to find out the next chapter in this dream sequence about the giant wolf that had nearly killed him.

The dreams seemed to give him a more positive outlook, uplifting his spirits, which had been beginning to falter. No longer did he brood about revenge or look upon himself with pity. Upon awakening each morning, he felt a surge of strength and power that became more evident as the days progressed. He knew he was healing not only physically but also mentally and spiritually, a clear gift from the Great Spirit that he couldn't deny.

Because of the recent dreams, he began to let go of the hate and the wish for vengeance against the giant wolf. Isha felt as if a dark, heavy weight had been lifted from him. He was almost approaching the sensation of joy. It seemed that the Great Spirit was showing him the giant wolf's life to rid him of his anger. He realized that hate, anger, and vengeance are burdens that men should not carry if they wish to live a good life.

After Isha was discharged from the hospital, he and Aingan walked down to the lake, where the canoe had been packed by Aingan and readied for the return trip. Isha walked slowly with a cane and refused help from his uncle. It was painful and stiff, but he was determined to make it without help. Aingan was uncharacteristically patient and walked at a slow pace, ready to catch his nephew if he stumbled. Isha was proud when he reached the canoe. It was a small victory, but it gave him hope for the future.

Winnipeg was a place Aingan and Isha never wanted to return to. During his stay in the city, Isha thought this must be the way wolves feel when encountering humankind. Like a wolf, Isha felt overwhelmed and intimidated by what he felt were the near magical machines of the white world. He thought of how the giant wolf must have felt about guns and man's other "magical devices." He and Aingan felt like lone wolves, who usually do not fare well in nature without their supporting pack.

When they finally got into the canoe and looked back at the city, both men felt a sense of relief. The canoe softly gliding through the water and the vast green forest ahead of them were things they were familiar with. This had a calming effect, giving them an immediate sense of freedom and self-worth. They were heading into the bush, a realm they felt was theirs, where they would feel the presence of the Great Spirit and comfort once again.

Return to a New Reality

During their long trip back to Lake Kashapon, Isha and his uncle sat by a campfire after having dinner. Aingan said to his nephew, "When you heal up and get stronger, the tribe will form a war party to attack this giant wolf. I'd like to skin his hide and tack it to Angus's trading-post wall for all to see. We can shoot them, trap them, and even use poison to rid the area of those killers."

Isha stared calmly into the fire while turning some burning embers over with a long stick and said, "Thanks, uncle, but I've had enough of war to last me a lifetime." He then told Aingan the long story of his powerful dreams. Aingan became silent, seemingly greatly affected by the tale Isha told. He no longer spoke of the giant wolf.

Upon returning from the long and arduous journey from Winnipeg, Isha went to see Tiskigapon. He knocked on the door of the tiny cabin and heard the squeaky little voice from within call, "Come in, Isha." Isha opened the door and entered her dimly lit, tidy abode.

"How did you know it was me?"

"I could tell by the sound of your footsteps. You always had a quick step, but now with a slight limp. Plus I've been expecting you. You've learned much in the last year, haven't you?"

"I have."

"Sit down and I'll make some Labrador tea for us. Talk is always better with a cup of tea. I heard about your harrowing ordeal with the wolves and your dog Atu. As you know, I did warn you about the Seal River country to the north and its negative presence."

"Yes, you did warn me, and I now believe you. I did find the giant black rock that you said was there."

Her eyes lit up as if they had fire behind them. She quickly leaned forward, almost as an automatic reflex of a young woman, seemingly losing seventy years of age within an instant. With a burning intensity, she looked at Isha's face. She asked, "Did you feel the power of the rock?"

"Oh yes, very much so."

Tiskigapon smiled and slowly leaned back in her chair, the fire slowly dying from her eyes, seemingly satisfied and returning to her old age. She ambled over to the stove and slowly brewed the tea as she asked him about his family and his experience in Winnipeg.

"I have some questions about some strange but vivid dreams while I was in the hospital," Isha said.

Tiskigapon brought the tea in tiny rough wooden cups and sat across from Isha on one of her miniature chairs. She placed her hands on the table and stared at Isha. "Tell me about the dreams," she said, looking at him as if she could see the inner workings of his soul.

Isha told her in story form of the dreams about the life of the giant wolf, including names of the animals. Tiskigapon looked as if she were hanging on every word with great interest. After Isha had finished the long and complex story of the vivid dreams, she replied, "This is a great honor that has been bestowed upon you by the Great Spirit! What you experienced were not mere dreams but a vision from beyond. Upon waking, did it feel like you were returning from another world with power, and was your mind clear afterward?"

"Yes, very much so."

"Dreams may be sent by the Great Spirit, but frequently they are cluttered with our other thoughts, making them difficult to understand. The Great Spirit wishes his will to be perfectly clear. He is explaining his actions to you by showing the wolves in a sympathetic, humanlike way. I have never heard of this happening. Your vision has great power. The Seal River country and the great wolf Mohegan are not to be disturbed while you or he is alive. I think you have felt this in your heart already."

"Yes, I have."

"The Great Spirit must have great plans for you and the giant wolf since he spared both of your lives. This giant wolf, Mohegan, must be very special. He is not quite an animal but exhibits intelligence and has many humanlike qualities. It will be for the next generation to explore this region to the north, but until then it is to be left alone. This will be the time of the wolf in the Seal River country, as it will be your time in this village upon Lake Kashapon. Both of you displayed great heroism and both experienced profound pain. The experience of courage together with great, painful loss tends to promote wisdom. I think this is how the Great Spirit is preparing both of you for something great in the future."

Tiskigapon leaned back from the table, sipped her hot tea, and smiled. She returned the conversation to more mundane topics of cooking and village life. Isha finished his tea and thanked Tiskigapon as he arose from the miniature table, ducking his head so as not to hit the rafters of the tiny cabin.

After several days thinking about what Tiskigapon had said, he walked to Angus McDonald's trading post, accompanied by Atu. The villagers greeted them both. Many people, especially children, came up to Atu wanting to pet the big dog, which Atu seemed to enjoy immensely. By the time Isha and Atu arrived at the trading post, they had a large entourage of well-wishers.

As Isha pushed the heavy log door open, he turned and waved to the villagers. As he shut the door, he immediately felt the warm, cozy atmosphere with the ever-present subtle aroma of coffee brewing and the sweet smell of pipe tobacco. From behind the counter, Angus gave a huge ear-to-ear smile.

"Isha! How are you?" He rushed from around the counter and gave his friend a big hug. "By golly, it's good to see you. I heard you had returned from Winnipeg. You'll have to tell me about it."

"I wish to thank you, Angus, for saving my life. The doctors in Winnipeg were impressed with your work."

"Sit down, Isha, and let me see where they worked on you." Isha sat down on a chair, pulled up his pant leg, and took off his shirt. Angus pulled up a chair and palpated the surgical sites, which were now well healed.

"It doesn't even hurt when you push on it," Isha said.

"Oh my, this is wonderful! This is better than I expected. They did a superb job," Angus said.

"I'd like to talk with you about some dreams I've had. Tiskigapon called them a vision."

"It's not uncommon to have nightmares after such a traumatic experience."

"No, it's not like that." Isha went on to tell Angus about the vision regarding Mohegan and the other animals that had been given to him in a sequence, like chapters in a book. "I talked with Tiskigapon about this. She feels they are a message from the Great Spirit."

"I wouldn't doubt that. There is a story in the first chapter of the Bible about a man named Joseph. He underwent many terrible events in his life as a young man. He was falsely accused of a crime and spent years as a slave and then in prison. Because of his abilities, constant positive attitude, and unshakable faith in God, he eventually became the most powerful man in the country next to the king. He was able to save his family and many others from starvation because of his elevated position. He couldn't have done this unless he'd suffered through those terrible experiences that gave him insight, wisdom, and subsequently forgiveness of the many people who had abused him. Through great wisdom he understood that retaining anger is not what God wants us to do.

"The Almighty many times will turn something bad into good. Quite possibly he will do the same for you. I feel confident that your ordeal will become a great learning experience and that better days are ahead for you. I do believe one thing is important for you: always remember that anger and hate will eventually destroy the vessel that contains them. It is best to let all that go. I would not dwell on the giant wolf as a target for vengeance. This is what makes humans different from animals—the ability to forgive people who have wronged us or, in your case, the giant wolf. Unfortunately, most human beings don't realize this, and in effect we are not that different from animals in many respects."

"I believe what you say, Angus. I understood this from the vision

I had in the hospital, but it's good to hear you say it. You're a source of great wisdom. One more thing I'd like to ask. What are potatoes and onions?"

"Oh my, that's about all I used to eat when I was a young lad back in Scotland. They are plants that grow underground like fat roots. They're quite common in the white world."

"I love them!" Isha said.

Angus replied, "It's funny you bring that up because I was thinking about shipping some up from Winnipeg. The good thing about both of those items is that they store well and can be eaten months after you receive them if stored in a cool environment, which would not be a problem around here. You don't have to thresh and prepare them like wild rice."

Isha was silent as he pondered what Angus had said. He didn't mention how he came to experience fried potatoes and onions. Angus knelt and rubbed Atu's head.

"I see you've healed well, my friend."

Atu seemed to give a lopsided, crooked smile from his deformed face.

It took approximately a year for Isha to fully recover from his ordeal. It was a miracle that he had survived. Isha later said that he willed himself to live, to fight for survival every day despite the overwhelming urge to let go and enter the spirit world, where there would be no pain. Angus and Aingan both said that Isha's "life force" was very strong. They had both seen men with much lesser injuries give up and slip away. While Isha was recovering, Aingan and other villagers hunted and provided food for him and his family.

The Aftermath and Understanding

Atu recovered from his wounds but was terribly disfigured. He'd lost an eye and one of his ears. He had a deep, gaping scar from one side of his face to the nose, which was split in two, resulting in two large and wide-open nostrils. Large areas of his torso were devoid of hair where large segments of his skin and muscle had been bitten off. Atu's facial and body deformities, instead of being considered ugly, were a badge of honor, like medals for a soldier. Upon seeing Isha and Atu in the village, Aingan knelt by Atu, putting their heads side by side, and laughed as he said, "Look, Atu's face looks almost like mine!"

Isha laughed and said, "All I see are two animals!"

Atu was revered and respected above all other dogs. He became a pet to the entire community and was treated exceptionally well by all. Atu walked freely around the village and was frequently given snacks and rubs on the head. Atu was thought of not as a dog but as a brave Cree warrior who had done an exceptionally brave thing by saving a fellow warrior's life.

Atu seemed to enjoy his newfound respect. He in turn was playful and well behaved with all the villagers. In a strange, doglike way, he seemed to always have a smile on his damaged face. Atu changed the villagers' attitude toward dogs in general. They came to see in most dogs what Isha and Angus had seen all along, and most reevaluated their method of training their sled dogs and adopted more positive ways.

Even after his recovery Isha still walked with a slight limp and couldn't run as swiftly as before his ordeal. He was unable to raise his left arm above his head, and his left-hand grip strength was slightly diminished but still functional. He had occasional discomfort throughout the rest of his life, but not enough to prevent him from doing what he had to do. He was able to return to his previous activities of providing for his family, hunting, fishing, and trapping without difficulty.

In the fall after returning from Winnipeg, Isha, accompanied by his good friend Atu, made the twenty-mile trip along his old trapline trail, retracing his harrowing run through the bush while being chased by Mohegan and the pack. At the end of the trail, he viewed the small ravine where the ambush had taken place and the exact spot where he and Mohegan had faced off in deadly combat. Isha found his rifle, canvas tarp, cooking utensils, beaver hat, mittens, and musk ox blanket, which had been left at the site of the battle. The wooden stock of the rifle had been gnawed nearly to splinters. The steel barrel of the gun was scored by deep scratches and teeth marks. The canvas tarp, hat, mittens, and musk ox blanket had been torn to shreds. The metal cooking utensils had deep dents and were deformed from the jaws of the wolves.

Anything with the scent of the hated man on it had been destroyed or damaged. Even the shelter had been torn down and destroyed. The wooden poles used for the inside of the tepee had been gnawed into pieces, and large splinters of shredded wood were scattered around the former campsite. Isha surmised that after the giant wolf had returned, having failed to kill his hated prey in his malignant, obsessive quest for revenge, he had taken out his rage on anything associated with man. When Isha looked at what had been done, he shivered at the thought of the ferocity and anger it had taken for the giant wolf and his pack to inflict such damage.

Isha walked around the area and saw the intact skeletal remains of the two wolves he had killed with his knife, one of whom was Wachak. The bones had lain undisturbed by wolves or other predators, which was quite unusual. Mohegan had probably placed his scent on the two dead animals, in effect saying, *Stay away from these two dead heroes.* Their bodies were not to be desecrated. Atu sniffed the bones and immediately recoiled, giving a small growl. He raised his head and looked around the area with the hair on his back bristling with alarm. Isha rubbed Atu's head and reassured him, "Everything is fine, Atu. We're in no danger."

Isha looked pensively out over the lake into the territory of the giant wolf, reflecting on his life-threatening experience. He thought man and wolf had many things in common. In fact, he thought man and wolf were kindred spirits. They were both predators that depended on others of their kind to work as a coordinated unit to plan and bring down their prey. Isha and his tribe went on a communal caribou hunt each year. The tribe planned out their strategy of attack much as a wolf pack did. Isha had personally seen the pack playing out similar tactics against him.

Man and wolf both devise complex hunting strategies. Both species are devoted parents who play with and teach their young. There is close camaraderie among members of the pack, who share food and friendship. Humans and wolves live in family groups that communicate and cooperate with others. Both have territories that they aggressively defend against outsiders, often destroying their enemies. Both care for their injured and elderly. Only a few other species exhibit these traits as clearly as wolves and humans do.

While Isha had been in the hospital, he had met several men who had been terribly wounded in wars of the British empire, which included Canada. Many had been wounded in the Great War, World War I. Isha had seen many young men who were more severely damaged than he was. Many had amputations, while others were disfigured and unable to function normally for the remainder of their lives. Some of the wounded men had tried to describe artillery fire and bombs, which Isha had no concept of aside from the obvious devastation they inflicted on human beings. Isha thought white men were able to harness thunder and lightning as weapons against their enemies. The wounded men's descriptions of their experiences were horrifying, yet none of the men seemed to harbor hate or resentment for their enemy. Isha thought, *Maybe the Great Spirit visited them in their dreams as well.*

Isha was told that one nation had sought revenge on another for the assassination of a prince. Then other nations had taken sides, even though they barely had any grievance against the initial countries involved in the war. Millions had been killed and injured in revenge for someone they didn't know or to protect small pieces of their territory. He realized that wars were frequently inadvertent or accidental catastrophes triggered by some unforeseen or unplanned event with horrible consequences. Even his own tribe had gone to war in the past on different occasions with the Ojibwa, Dene, and Inuit peoples. He thought how different men were from animals. He thought men were probably worse. Isha remembered his conversation with Angus about men frequently being dumb as sheep, led by wicked or incompetent leaders, with individuals losing the capacity to think for themselves. Isha hadn't understood at the time, but now he saw the results of men being led into a meaningless war.

He realized that war was sometimes a necessary evil but oftentimes was not.

Isha knew he had precipitated the attack by the giant wolf. This implied that the giant wolf had self-awareness and even love for a permanent mate, or one could say a wife. These characteristics were something most people thought of as uniquely human. Isha now knew that wolves were not much different from humans.

Isha began to respect the giant wolf in a strange but primitive way, one hunter to another. He began to understand the situation and why it had occurred. He would never intentionally kill or purposely trap another wolf. He felt that they were higher beings, capable of humanlike traits and possessing greater intelligence than most other animals. Isha would not wage another war with Mohegan. There was plenty of land for both to hunt.

Isha's wife had a healthy baby boy. After several years Isha became the tribal chief and was renowned for his good leadership and wisdom. He had no more significant dreams or encounters with wolves. He never trapped or hunted in the territory of Mohegan again, nor did any other villagers, for fear of the giant wolf. It would be up to the next generation to return to the Seal River country if they wished. In the 1960s Isha's son began trapping the Seal River country, bringing back a bounty of valuable furs. He never had problems with wolves. He occasionally saw them, but they never bothered him. Isha's son built a cabin close to the giant black rock, which again became a sacred place for the tribe. No one else experienced any of the visual phenomena that Isha had seen while sitting on the giant black rock. Most people of the tribe believed that the negative force that had previously been present in the region was now gone.

Isha thought it was his fate to be killed by wolf attack if he ventured into the Seal River country. He felt that the Great Spirit had warned him in dreams not to go. However, he was determined to explore the region no matter what the signs. He realized that the Great Spirit had brought Atu to him to change his fate and spare his life.

The attack by the wolves gave Isha a deeper understanding of the relationship between wolves and humans. He concluded that humans and wolves had evolved through time together and were kindred spirits. Through Isha's traumatic experience, he thought the main difference was humans' ability to forgive and dispel vengeance to live a happier life. However, he realized that under the thin veneer of human civilization lies the wolf within us all. This greater understanding was possible only because Isha had survived the REVENGE OF THE WOLF.

Bruce D. Graham M.D. is a board certified General and Colon Rectal surgeon who lives in Shawnee, Kansas. He is married and has three children. He received a B.A. at the University of Missouri where he was also a collegiate wrestler. He received an M.S. at the University of Arkansas and an M.D. at the University of Missouri. His General Surgery and fellowship in Colon and Rectal Surgery training was at Michigan State University. He has been in private practice in the Kansas City area for over thirty years has been an associate clinical professor at the University of Kansas. He has published numerous scientific papers. Also the author of Life Lessons and Spirit of the Wilderness, he is an amateur historian, an avid fisherman, and gardener.

www.ingramcontent.com/pod-product-compliance
Lightning Source LLC
Jackson TN
JSHW050312110725
87393JS00011B/77